Act French

Contemporary Plays from France

Act French

Contemporary Plays from France

EDITED, WITH AN INTRODUCTION, BY
PHILIPPA WEHLE

PAJ PUBLICATIONS
New York

Act French: Contemporary Plays from France is published by PAJ Publications, P.O. Box 532, Village Station, New York, N.Y. 10014.

PAJ Publications is distributed to the trade by Consortium Book Sales and Distribution: www.cbsd.com
General Editor of PAJ Publications: Bonnie Marranca

Design: Susan Quasha
Front cover image: Pierre Huyghe, *Les Grands Ensembles,* 1994/2001
Vistavision transferred to Digi Beta and DVD, 8 minutes
Courtesy of the artist and Marian Goodman Gallery, New York

Publication of this book has been made possible in part with funds provided by the Cultural Services of the French Embassy in the United States, and FACE (French American Cultural Exchange).

LIBRARY OF CONGRESS CATALOGING-IN-PUBLICATION DATA

Act French : contemporary plays from France / edited with an introduction by Philippa Wehle.
p. cm.
ISBN-13: 978-1-55554-078-4
ISBN-10: 1-55554-078-3
1. French drama—21st century—Translations into English. I. Wehle, Philippa.
PQ1240.E5A38 2007
812'.9208—dc22

2007026999

First Edition, 2007
Printed in the United States of America

Contents

Acknowledgments

I would like to express my profound gratitude to Emmanuelle de Montgazon, former Cultural Attaché of the Cultural Services of the French Embassy in New York City, who welcomed the idea of an anthology of contemporary plays from France and gave her full support to this project. Thanks as well to Nicole Birmann Bloom, Program Coordinator, Dance and Theatre Office of the Cultural Services of the French Embassy, for her valuable help and support throughout this project. I am also indebted to Etant donnés, the French-American Fund for the Performing Arts, for generous grants received in 2004, 2005, and 2006, supporting the translations of José Pliya's *We Were Sitting on the Shores of the World* ... and Philippe Minyana's *Inventories*, as well as the staged readings of these plays at the Ohio Theatre, New York City.

I am most grateful to the authors and translators of the plays in this volume who without exception greeted my requests to publish their work with generosity and encouragement. To Ellen Lampert-Gréaux, co-translator of *We Were Sitting on the Shores of the World* ..., special thanks for her many valuable suggestions. A special tribute to Emmanuelle Marie, the author of *Cut*, who despite her battle with cancer took time out to talk with me about her work and give me permission to publish *Cut*. She died May 10, 2007, at the age of 42. I know that she would have been happy to see this book published.

To Robert Lyons, Artistic Director, and Erich Jungwirth, Producing Director, and their dedicated crew at the Ohio Theatre, my gratitude for making these staged readings a success; and Vincent Colin, director of the José Pliya and Philippe Minyana readings at the Ohio Theatre, for helping to make these translations flow naturally on the stage, and especially to Robert Lyons, for helping make *Inventories* colloquially fluent. My gratitude as well to Stephanie Klapper, director of Klapper Casting, for her excellent choices of actors for these staged readings. Their contributions to the final translations were invaluable.

A word of thanks also to George Hunka, copy editor of the *Act French* volume, for his patience and understanding. Heartfelt appreciation to my dear friends and family, Lucienne DeWulf, Lenora Champagne, Judith Johnson, Judith G. Miller, and Edith Wehle, whose wisdom and guidance have been invaluable to my completion of this project.

The Power of Words

Philippa Wehle

"Words fly, disrupting the space, crossing and filling it.
The air quivers with words hurled, beaten, or devoured . . . "

Hugues Le Tanneur
Le Monde, November 19, 2003

Act French, a season of new theatre from France, took place in New York City from July through December, 2005. It was conceived by the Cultural Services of the French Embassy in New York and AFAA (Association Française d'Action Artistique) to offer New York audiences varied opportunities to discover new French playwriting and performance. Dozens of established and emerging playwrights were produced on New York's stages, from the Brooklyn Academy of Music to the Ohio Theatre in Soho, some in French, others in English translation. There were readings as well as full productions, symposia, lectures, and films, all reflecting the vibrancy of new writing from the French-language stage.

Act French: Contemporary Plays from France cannot begin to capture the wealth and variety of today's French theatre as presented over a six-month period in New York by Act French. Nonetheless the authors and plays presented here have been chosen in keeping with the aims and spirit of that event. Two plays received full productions in translation at the festival (Olivier Cadiot's *A. W.O.L.* and Valère Novarina's *Adramelech's Monologue*). *We Were Sitting on the Shores of the World . . .,* by José Pliya, was given a staged reading as part of a week-long celebration of his theatre. The work of Philippe Minyana and Michèle Sigal was discussed and excerpts were performed at the New York Public Library series. Emmanuelle Marie's *Cut* would have been part of the festival if a theatre could have been found to produce it. The most notable and egregious absence from the Act French program, however, was Michel Vinaver's powerful *11 September 2001*, produced by CalArts with actors from the CalArts School of Theatre, directed by French director Robert Cantarella and presented by REDCAT. It was slated to be on the roster but was unfortunately canceled for political reasons. It is therefore my pleasure to include in this volume one of France's most distinctive living playwright's perspective on the September 11 events.

The Act French festival program embraced numerous writing styles, from more traditional dialogue-based works, such as Jean-Marie Besset's *Commentaire d'amour* and Jean-Claude Grumberg's *L'Atelier*, to more exploratory works, such as Pascal Rambert's *Paradise (Unfolding Time)*, "an experiment in expelling the text by pushing it to the periphery." Although one cannot speak of any one specifically French style of writing, it is possible to identify a certain way of using language, its rhythms, sounds, and poetry, that seems to be prevalent among many of today's French-language authors. "We have moved from a theatre of action," says Michel Azama, author of *From Godot to Zucco: An Anthology of French-language Playwrights*, "to a theatre of the spoken word." Plays from France are frequently propelled first and foremost by language. Gone are the linear plots, the idea of the character as a clearly defined entity, continuity, and logical conclusions. Following in the footsteps of Beckett and Ionesco, but even more determined to do away with characters and action in the classical sense, the new French theatre favors fragmentation, disruption, ellipsis, and digression, and, like challenging puzzles to be pieced together, it may leave audiences disarmed and confronted with questions. Clearly, France is experiencing an exciting period of new dramatic writing. With the exception of Ariane Mnouchkine, who brought her extraordinary Théâtre du Soleil with their epic production of *Le dernier caravansérail, Odyssées* to the festival, the age of the director-as-superstar, the hallmark of French theatre in the 1970s and 1980s, is over.

This interest in the word, in speech and sounds, in rhythm and musicality rather than plot, character, and dialogue, is shared by the authors in this anthology. Olivier Cadiot's delusional protagonist in *A.W.O.L.*, an adaptation by Marion Schoevaert of Cole Swensen's translation of the Cadiot novel *Le Colonel Zouave* (published as *Colonel Zoo* in the Green Integer edition), is a lone voice crying out to an indifferent world with a furious whirlwind of words. Whether a butler in *Colonel Zoo* or (in Schoevaert's adaptation) a homeless man wandering the streets of New York, subjected to the taunting jibes of an all-male chorus who play Wall Street brokers, he is a man obsessed by hourly tasks. He choreographs lists of his "duties" and how to perform them. "No problem…," he tells himself. "Take two steps back. Freeze. At ease." He is so caught up in his performance that he slips into fantasies of himself as would-be lover planning an affair with a beautiful redhead, as a spy listening in on secret discussions with important people, as a colonel leading his men under the hail of projectiles, and finally as a war hero. He delivers his monologue of shifting roles in different voices and registers—focused, serious, breathless, and confidential—according to the identities of his invented characters.

Valère Novarina's monologist Adramelech, the Drama King (from *Melech* in Hebrew and *Malik* in Arab, which both translate as "King"), also conjures many different personas in his lengthy monologue which appears in the middle of Novarina's novel *Le Babil des classes dangereuses* (*Babble of the Dangerous Classes*), a monologue that has frequently been performed as a play in itself. Adramelech tells stories about his childhood and the wars he has been through, along with tales of his many crimes. He appeals to former classmates, crosses the French Alps, imitates the Bible, and comes close to becoming a prophet. Novarina's objective is to explode language, to investigate its roots, and ultimately to create a new language. In his theatre, words—not ordinary words, but invented words, truncated words, unfamiliar words with hidden etymological roots, words based on alliterations—pulsate in an avalanche of sounds and images. Novarina's theatre is clearly a "Theatre of the Ears," to borrow the title of a play for recorded voice and electronic puppet, developed around his work at CalArts in 1999. "Sufferin' sycophant!" Adramelech shouts, as he begins to tell his life's story. "Sufferin' sulfurous supine simian syllogist!" Such resplendent texts are a pleasure to read, but, as Novarina insists, they need the actor's body and voice to be fully realized.

Philippe Minyana is also fascinated by words—everyday, familiar words. His characters, some nameless, some identified only by their first names, are ordinary people sharing their seemingly humdrum lives in a flow of punctuation-free prose. In contrast to Cadiot's and Novarina's monologists, those of Minyana live in a clear sociological context and determined time. In fact, Minyana favors the use of real-life interviews or newspaper items as the starting point for many of his plays. With these raw materials, he structures a language without designated vocal pauses, reflecting the breathless, halting delivery of real people caught in a confessional mode. His characters, however, are not real people. They are composites that allow the playwright to give voice to individuals whose social condition is at or close to the bottom of the scale: factory workers, women on welfare, and other marginalized individuals.

In *Inventories,* for example, three women—Jacqueline, Angèle, and Barbara—are invited to participate in a television show to which they must each bring their most treasured object and talk about it. Jacqueline brings her favorite wash basin; Angèle, her 1954 dress; and Barbara, a standing lamp bought years before at the Galeries Lafayette. Before long, the women are exposing every grim detail of lives gone awry. Their monologues, spoken to the audience with little awareness of what they or the other women are saying, take the form of a talking marathon that reveals the most intimate details of each woman's life, their insecurities as well as their dreams. Their candid and moving confessions are both comic and sad. Minyana reveals these tragedies of ordinary lives in a language that is fragmented, disjointed, and frenetic. His is a theatre of "linguistic stunning," to borrow a term used by Mary Noonan in an essay for a 2007 issue of the *Yale French Review.*

Language—elegant, lyrical, radiant—is equally central to the work of Franco-Beninese writer José Pliya, a member of a new generation of African-born writers who do not define themselves as "African," but rather seek to be understood as "universal." Born in Benin, West Africa, educated in the French lycée in Niger and recipient of a Doctorate in Letters from the University of Paris, Pliya is currently director of l'Artchipel, the National Theatre of Guadeloupe. It is no wonder that he sees himself as an author between multiple worlds whose focus is not on specific social or political issues, but rather on the fundamental evil in man, regardless of color, gender, or background, and the eternal themes of exile and belonging, of loss, loyalty, and love.

Pliya favors simple, intimate stories. His characters—a man, a woman, a mother—are "wanderers" caught up in irreconcilable conflicts which are often brutal, sensual, and powerfully disturbing. In *We Were Sitting on the Shores of the World . . . ,* for example, a woman and a man meet by chance on a beach. The woman, a native of the island who has moved away, has come home for a visit. The man claims ownership for the entire beach and insists that she leave. Despite her protests that she was born on this island and used to play on the beach as a child, he sees her as a stranger who has forfeited her right to enjoy the pleasure of her birthplace. Under a harsh and cruel sun, she makes one last attempt to engage the man in a dialogue, but he refuses and even threatens to rape her in order to demonstrate that he is right. Pliya addresses this gulf between a man and a woman, between the past and the present, in a metaphorical style inspired by the rhythms and musicality of the Creole language.

"Language is the only thing you hear" in radio plays, says Lucien Attoun, director with Micheline Attoun of Théâtre Ouvert, and producer of many radio dramas since 1969, speaking of the unique world of radio drama in France at the New York Public Library for the Performing Arts, Lincoln Center, as part of the Act French program. Thanks to France Culture (Radio France's cultural station that regularly commissions new plays), listeners can tune into seven hours of radio theatre every week and discover four or five new plays. In addition, more than 100 hours of radiophonic dramas are broadcast each week in 35 European countries, reaching 75 million listeners. Reaching a much wider audience than stage plays, radio theatre provides an immense theatre without walls, a forum of special appeal to today's French playwrights, many of whom write for radio.

Michèle Sigal, winner of the 2006 New Radio Talent prize awarded by the SACD (Société des Auteurs et Compositeurs Dramatiques) for her radio play *Pumpkin on the Air*, is among such authors. She is frequently commissioned to write plays for France Culture. An actress and author of several published and produced full-length plays, she finds that writing for radio is liberating. "It has broadened my palette and given my writing a new sensuality," she says. "Time and space, the relationship to the audience, the constraints, are completely different. You have to create mental images, be aware of a certain kind of musicality, go for a more lyrical type of writing, find the right tone, and especially, remain aware of your intimate relationship with the audience, an audience that must be actively involved in the creative act along with you."

Michèle Sigal's *Pumpkin on the Air* is a modern Cinderella tale in the form of a "radiophonic fiction," to borrow the term currently used by radio producers in France. Set in today's Paris with all of its socio-economic challenges—widespread unemployment, immigrant families living in squalor, victims of devastating fires, and Chinese immigrants hiding in a basement workroom—Sigal's fable imagines this urban landscape through the eyes and words of an eight-year-old girl, Juliette. Her father, an unemployed taxi driver, is so depressed that he spends his time listening to the radio, the only object he has salvaged from his taxi. Whenever he looks at reality, he sees butterflies before his eyes. Her mother is doing her best to cope realistically with their situation while Juliette retreats into a fantasy world, in which she imagines her father as a king who has lost his kingdom and whose chariot is reduced to pulp, the size of a pumpkin. Meanwhile, Mamadou Romeo, a street sweeper from Mali in search of his cousin, wanders the streets of Paris. Homeless and homesick, he finds himself forced to sleep in garbage cans and on subway cars. Inevitably, Juliette meets Romeo and they become friends, but theirs is a brief encounter as Romeo must find his cousin and Juliette must continue her imaginary tale in hopes of bringing her father back to reality.

Sigal's theatre deals with social and political tensions in today's world using a poetic language composed of novel wordplays, double meanings, and inventive images. When Romeo imagines that he sees an elephant wearing Africa on its back dreaming its nonchalant dream, the image is striking. It is his vision of Africa, his dream of the peace and calm of home. Later, however, when the elephant reappears and refuses to carry him back to Africa, Mamadou Romeo realizes that he cannot return to his homeland. Like his cousins and the other African immigrants, he will have to stay in one of Paris's dilapidated hotels, where so many have already been burned to death.

Because *Pumpkin on the Air* was written for radio, Sigal offers her listeners the pleasure of hearing the street sounds, the different accents, and the multinational voices of today's Paris. Brooms sweeping water in the gutters, the language spoken by the immigrants from Mali, fragments of sentences in Chinese, along with the exotic music of Mamadou Romeo's many names—from Mamadou Romeo to Mamadou Romeo Bankale Baba Baracouna—evoke the reality of the city's immigrant populations. These are the victims of ineffectual officials like "the Minister of Calamity, who is the first to arrive at the site of insanity to declare war on the fire," when the uninhabitable building has already burned. This may be a fairy tale with a happy ending (the father is cured), but there is no happy ending for the street sweepers from Mali or the illegal Chinese workers who have been found out by the immigration services.

Language used musically is also of primary interest to actress and writer Emmanuelle Marie, who frequently writes eloquently and openly of concerns specific to women: the special relationship they have to their bodies in *Cut*, for example, or their bonding around the death of their mother in *Blanc*. Hers is not so much a feminist perspective, however, as it is a sociological one.

In her play *Cut*, she creates a partita in dramatic form composed of the voices of three women who meet in a ladies' restroom and exchange their views about "it," the word they use for a woman's private parts. With no biography or psychology to define them, they are simply there to bear witness. Separate, together, or in unison, they form a chorus of women exploring their intimate fears and desires in a language that is both lyrical and incantatory. Sung softly or loudly, depending on the subject being discussed, their songs range from whispered confessions to hosannas of pleasure, from a litany of the strict rules handed down by conservative mothers to their daughters ("Close your legs! Tuck in your butt! And pray!") to a delightful description of the sexy, frilly clothes women are expected to wear to attract and please men. There is nothing vulgar about their discussion; on the contrary. Their conversation is both serious and amusing as they "sing" the praises of peeing sitting down, for example, which, in contrast to the standing position of men, provides women with moments of calm and solitude, a chance to achieve a brief state of grace or discuss their relationships with their mothers, with men, with each other.

Michel Vinaver's dramas of shifting perspectives, and his artistic practice of using seemingly ordinary language transformed through a technique of collage and montage, are well known. In the weeks following the devastating destruction of the Twin Towers, he wrote *11 September 2001* in American English (his phrase) as a personal meditation on the events of 9/11. "All the world was witness to this live event," notes Vinaver, "the shock was amazing—with reverberations that blinded us all." Constructed as a dramatic oratorio with thematic arias, choral parts, and recitatives, the voices of the catastrophe—witnesses, political figures, terrorists, and reporters—intermingle and reverberate to present audiences with different points of view, emotional as well as ideological. Along with the words of Bush and Bin Laden are transmissions, accounts, and memories from those who were lost in the attack as well as those who survived. In order to capture the totality of this event, Vinaver includes documents from what was happening before the attacks as well as events that followed: excerpts from a speech by President Bush, for example, and a statement supposedly made by Osama Bin Laden at the time of the invasion of Afghanistan (October, 2001).

Using fragments of ordinary speech rearranged in such a way as to build a mosaic of possible readings rather than a realistic theatre of the everyday, his structuring of this material allows themes to emerge indirectly so that readers and spectators can receive this experience from different perspectives. For Vinaver, the theatre engages with the political realities of the day and the socio-economic struggles of ordinary people. Public and private concerns are inseparable for him. His textual cantata—a poetic collage—leaves it to the individual to see this attack and its many ramifications in all their complexity.

The authors of this volume, all artists of language, offer a fresh auditory experience, a distinctive writing style—disruptive, fragmentary, and provocative. We are either blown away by the overflow of words or drawn in by the mystery behind the pauses and silences. But mostly, these French voices speak to us from a distinctly French perspective.

What makes them "French"? Generally speaking, to these writers language is more important than dramaturgical issues. It is so important that noted French playwright Olivier Py has even written an entire play, *Epistle to Young Actors So That the Word May Be Restored to the Word,* in which he urges his readers to resurrect the miraculous powers of language. "The Word is the love that is embodied in speech in the form of a Promise," he tells them, and then proceeds to demonstrate his own verbal agility. Even in Vinaver's theatre (in which, Py contends, "what is unsaid weighs more than what is said"), it is the way he uses snippets of spoken language as his raw material and his particular method of composition, with its discontinuities, dissonances, repetitions, and variations, that sparks our interest more than the story that is being told.

This is not to say that contemporary French theatre is not richly varied and constantly evolving. The critic Judith Miller convincingly argues that the theatre that matters in today's France is a transnational one reflecting the new France, which is "multicultural, destabilized, and embattled by the rapid movement of populations and the shifting balance in world power." However, she is speaking specifically of the theatres of Ariane Mnouchkine and Peter Brook, with their blendings of nationalities and texts borrowed from sacred Hindu writings, for example, in the case of Brook's *Mahabharata*, or collectively created from interviews with refugees by Mnouchkine's company, which is currently composed largely of non-French actors. This is certainly one possible reading of what is happening in theatre in France today, but it leaves out the importance of the written dramatic text in the more conventional sense. Tom Sellar, editor-in-chief of Yale's *Theater*, has voiced a different reading, one that is based, interestingly, on his experience of the Act French festival offerings: "A preoccupation with language—its form and its function in society and the imagination—remains very much at the center of French theatre. This is surprising, more than 50 years after the great experiments of literary modernism and in a time when artists and audiences are deeply skeptical about the power of words." This "faith in the theatrical capacity of language," as he calls it, is, I believe, what defines the work of contemporary French-language playwrights today.

In the fall of 2005, the French government (through its cultural agencies) sponsored and gave generous support to the Act French festival in order to offer an "illuminating, bridge-building vision of contemporary French culture and spark lively, curative dialogues" between leading theatre artists, patrons, and professionals of France and the United States. To the extent possible in a limited time period, Act French achieved this mission. Today, France has a new president, Nicolas Sarkozy, who during his campaign threatened to eliminate the Ministry of Culture and Communication altogether, and showed little interest in the kind of cultural exchange that would promote the work of France's most inventive artists—artists such as the ones in this anthology, whose experimental use of language creates new linguistic possibilities that are at opposite ends of the straightforward, direct, provocative rhetoric of the new president. Will there be a possibility of cultural renewal under the new French government? Will theatre as an art form decline in the face of conservatism? These questions hang in the air. The authors in this volume, directly (as in the case of Vinaver, for whom theatre must be engaged with the social and political realities of the day, or Michèle Sigal, who grounds her plays in the social and political issues of today's world) or indirectly (as with Pliya, Novarina, and others, who create plays in which the personal is political and the individual implies the general), are all telling us that a new theatrical language has to be found and voiced dramatically in order to resist the conservatism of the nation's social, political, and cultural life.

A word about translation: It goes without saying that translation of any important text is always a challenging task. On a scale of difficulty, however, translating poetic texts is the highest. Suffice it to say that beyond the already difficult challenge of remaining true to the authors' words, the translators in this volume have masterfully captured the musicality, intonations, rhythms, and sensorial qualities of the works presented here. It is thanks to their special gifts as artists of the word that these plays can be appreciated by an English-speaking audience.

We Were Sitting on the Shores of the World . . .

José Pliya

Translated by Philippa Wehle, with the help of Ellen Lampert Gréaux.

CHARACTERS

The Woman
The Man
The Female Friend
The Male Friend

The Woman: Oh, sir. Sir. Have you seen my friends? We were supposed to meet on this beach, for a picnic, around noon. I'm a little late and I'm surprised they're not here.

The Man: No, miss. I haven't seen your friends. I've been lying here on the beach for several hours and I haven't seen anybody. This beach is quite remote. Nobody ever comes here. I haven't seen your friends.

The Woman: I'm surprised. My friends told me to meet them here. They know how to get here better than I do since I don't live here. I'm just visiting. My friends are always on time. They should have been here already. I'm surprised.

The Man: Understandably. But I'm telling you they haven't come. They aren't here and it's not likely, not likely at all, that they would come this far. This is a private beach. They couldn't have told you to meet them here. Believe me, they won't come. Not to this beach.

The Woman: These are the shores of the world, aren't they? I didn't have much trouble finding them. I recognized them. I recognized them right away. They *haven't* changed.

The Man: These aren't the shores of the world any more. Your friends should have told you that. This beach has been bought. You can't stay here. I'm sorry.

The Woman: I must insist, if you don't mind. First of all, my friends were very clear about spending the day here, not any place else. Furthermore, just a little while ago, while I was getting lost trying to find this place, I ran into an old man on the side of the highway. He was wearing a straw hat and he pointed out this beach and not any other.

The Man: What more can I say? Your friends aren't here and I repeat, they won't be coming. The old man in the straw hat couldn't have sent you here. He probably pointed to some other beach with his shaky finger, a beach up there or another one down below. But not this one. No, not this one.

The Woman: Forgive my confusion. I wouldn't want to doubt your word. You're from around here. I can see that and I can hear it too. You must be right. Still, if you don't see any harm in it, I'm going to wait a few more minutes. I'm going to wait for my friends. If you don't mind.

The Man: You're wasting your time. They won't come and you can't stay here. You don't have the right. You can go wait for them up there, a little farther away, but not here, no, not here. *(A beat.)*

The Woman: The beach is still as beautiful as ever, with its powdery sand and blue ocean stretching all the way to the horizon, and the sky reflecting that same brightness. It's still as beautiful as ever.

The Man: We try. That's true. Ever since we've owned it, we try to protect it. We have to keep it clean, maintain it, and watch out for the tides. And of course, keep foreign women from coming here, using it and swimming, whenever they get lost and want to take over the beach, which happens from time to time.

THE WOMAN: I understand. I was born here, you know. I spent my first years on the golden sands of this beach. I used to live right behind here, up toward that hill. I remember a beach filled with people. We would run into each other on Sundays, at Easter time, at family picnics. Even though there were huge crowds, I remember the beach was clean.

THE MAN: Times change. The country has changed. People don't respect beaches anymore. They're dirty and black. They're not well-maintained and you find the wrong kind of people on them. Listen, your friends should have warned you, you shouldn't, really you shouldn't wander onto a beach around here by yourself. It's dangerous. There are men prowling around in the dunes. It's dangerous. *(A beat.)*

THE WOMAN: Would you have a light?

THE MAN: A light?

THE WOMAN: Yes, a light. I'd like to smoke a cigarette while I'm waiting for them. *(A beat.)*

THE MAN: You're going to smoke?

THE WOMAN: Yes. *(A beat.)*

THE MAN: A cigarette?

THE WOMAN: Yes. *(A beat.)*

THE MAN: Here, on this beach?

THE WOMAN: If you don't mind. *(A beat.)*

THE MAN: I think you don't understand, miss. This is a protected beach.

You can't stay here. You can't even walk across it. And you want to smoke? You haven't understood me at all.

The Woman: But, sir, just one cigarette. What harm is there in that? I'll use my left hand as an ashtray and I promise you, I'll keep the butt with me until I can throw it away later, when I've left your beach. I won't get it dirty.

The Man: You can't smoke here. It's not allowed. Don't insist. In any case, smoking while waiting for your friends is useless. It's a waste of time for you to stay here any longer. They won't come.

The Woman: Let's give them a little more time. Time enough for me to smoke a cigarette. That's not very long. Give me a light. I'll light my cigarette. I'll smoke it and if they haven't come during that time, I'll leave. I will leave.

The Man: No. Enough time to smoke a cigarette is already too much time. You should have left by now. You have to leave. Go back the way you came, along the little rocky path. When you get to your car, you'll find that old man in the straw hat. He'll give you a light. Go now. *(A beat.)*

The Woman: It's hot.

The Man: …

The Woman: You can really feel that sun beating straight down on our heads.

The Man: …

The Woman: I'm thirsty.

The Man: …

The Woman: Would you have something to drink?

THE MAN: ...

THE WOMAN: I see you have a cooler next to you. Would you have something to drink, sir?

THE MAN: Yes, I have a cooler with beer, fruit juice, ice, and water in it. I could offer you some, with the simple gesture of someone giving something to drink to a woman who's asked for it. But I won't. I won't give you anything to drink.

THE WOMAN: You want me to leave. Give me something to drink and I'll go. You hand me the drink. I'll take it and I'll say thank you. I'll open it as I start to leave and I'll drink it to quench my thirst. I'm really thirsty.

THE MAN: I won't give you anything to drink. I'm beginning to know you. I know that once you have the drink in your hands, you won't leave. Not right away, like I'm asking you to.

THE WOMAN: You don't know me. You've told me that the people I'm waiting for aren't going to come and I'm ready to believe you. I'm telling you that if you give me something to drink, I'll leave. You have to believe me.

THE MAN: I can't believe you any more because you're not keeping the one promise you made. You promised to leave and you aren't leaving. You want to smoke. You want to drink. You want to talk about this and that and stay on this beach where you're not authorized to stay. I don't believe you.

THE WOMAN: I wouldn't delay my departure if you'd just take the time to listen to me, to hear me and satisfy my request. I'm not asking you for beer, juice, or carbonated drinks, which aren't very refreshing anyway. You might refuse to give them to me, that's your right. I'm asking you for some water. You can't refuse that. You can't refuse me that.

THE MAN: It's not the water I'm refusing to give you—I've plenty of that in my cooler—it's the coolness that goes along with it, the coolness that belongs to me. That's quite precious and I'm afraid it might give you yet another pretext not to leave. That's what I'm afraid of. You can't have a drink. Not of my water. No, not of my water.

THE WOMAN: I find your position a bit excessive. Yes, that's the word, excessive. I'm not going to insist. I'm not going to insist any more. I'm leaving. *(A beat.)*

THE MAN: What are you doing?

THE WOMAN: It's hot. I'm going to take a swim.

THE MAN: Swim? Don't even think about it. That would mean you're going to get undressed here, on these shores, in front of me. That would mean that your clothes are going to be spread out on the sand while you're taking a swim. That's not allowed. Don't even think about it.

THE WOMAN: I'm thinking about it, sir, I'm thinking about it, and I really feel like doing it. I feel like getting undressed and putting my clothes, all of my clothes, there, on the beach. I feel like going into the ocean which must be warm or maybe even hot, but even so, it would cool me off. That's what I feel like doing, sir, before leaving.

THE MAN: You won't do that. I forbid you to do that. You're breaking the law. I was wrong to be welcoming and accept your presence here. That's it. I'm going to get up and come over to you. Before I get there, before I even get near you, you should be gone. That's it.

THE WOMAN: Do as you like, sir, go ahead. Come on over. Come right up to me and before you get here, I'll be gone from your beach, from your sand, from your shores, and into the ocean which, if I'm not mistaken, doesn't belong to you. You can't keep me from going into the ocean and staying there as long as I like. The ocean doesn't belong to you.

The Man: It's not the ocean and its wide open spaces that I forbid you to touch. It's the sand and the contact of your feet with the grains of sand. It's your clothes which you inevitably will put down on this beach which is mine and where you've left your footprints ever since you got here. I can't stand that. It's my beach and I forbid you to trample on it, you and the clothes you're wearing.

The Woman: If I understand you correctly, all I have to do is go into the ocean, fully dressed, just as I am right now, in order to make you happy. All I have to do to get you to be calm, to appease and soothe you, to get you to go back to your beach towel, which is spread out in the sun, is stop standing on your beach.

The Man: No. In order for me to get back my calm and return to my tanning, you're going to have to disappear, fully dressed, naked, half-dressed, or whatever you like, but you have to disappear. Only then will I be able to get back to my book and locate the sentence I was reading when you interrupted me.

The Woman: You're getting a bad deal, sir. If I take a swim with my clothes on, as you're suggesting, then I'll have to come out soaking wet and before leaving, I'll have to spread out my clothes on the sands of your beach and wait for them to dry. You're getting a bad bargain.

The Man: I'm not going to bargain with you. This is my place. I'm ordering you to leave. That's an order, miss. It's not a proposal that can be discussed. I'm not threatening you. It's an established fact that you must accept. Those are my orders. You're not welcome on my beach.

The Woman: I think I've understood that, sir. You are quite clear. I'm going to try to be equally clear so that we can be done with this. I'm going to take my clothes off. I'm going to put them down on the sand. I'm going to take a swim. After that, I'll leave.

The Man: You can't force your clothes on me, the ones you're going to throw on the sand so casually. You can't make me listen to those games you're going to play in the waves. You can't shock me with your nudity at high noon. You simply can't do that.

The Woman: My nudity bothers you? Then close your eyes. Turn your head away. Turn your back on me like sensitive men do. And if that's too much to ask, then keep your eyes wide open behind your dark glasses. That will create an illusion.

The Man: Don't misunderstand me. You are provoking me by getting undressed. Provoking me legitimizes my reaction, a reaction you don't know and which might surprise you. I must ask you: are you ready to experience my reaction? Are you ready?

The Woman: You couldn't possibly be more predictable than you already are. For reasons unknown to me, you took a dislike to me. As soon as I got here. Before I even said a word. Before I even appeared, you already knew that you didn't want me here, on the shores of the world. You don't scare me.

The Man: And you're right not to be afraid. I won't hurt you as long as you obey me, provided that you follow my orders and that you respect the discreet nature of this place and its one and only rule which is that you leave.

The Woman: You're in no position to give me orders. You've claimed that this is your place, your beach, but that doesn't give you the right to treat me this way. You haven't treated me with the slightest bit of decorum. I am a woman after all. I have the right to expect a minimum of courtesy but you refuse to give me any. I have a right to expect that.

The Man: No. You've got the wrong country. You've got the wrong island. You've got the wrong beach. We're not in one of those cold countries where you come from and where women demand that men pay them homage and give them compliments. This is my home. You're on my land and under my law.

The Woman: What law are you talking about? I'm looking around and I don't see any. I don't see anything written down, not in the wind, not on the sand. Nothing here proves to me that what you're saying is true. Nothing authorizes you to expose yourself naked on this shore and in front of me, so immodestly. I'm not complaining about your flashy beauty. I'm not offended by your seductive muscles and those indolent, lascivious ways you have.

The Man: Now that's precisely one of the reasons why I didn't want you to stay here. You're closing in on my intimacy. You're violating my secret beach. You undress me with your eyes and I can't stand that. And I also know that I'm going to hate your nudity, your contours, your curvaceousness, your roundness, and all those shapely features that you're going to inevitably exhibit. That's reason enough to justify my orders.

The Woman: I'm not convinced. Your reasons don't suit me. They aren't the real reasons why you want me to go. They sound false. It's the same with your authority. You know what they say: true authority doesn't allow for discussion, you just wield it and that's that. And you haven't been successful in doing that. You're hiding the truth from me. I won't leave until you tell me why I can't stay here, on the shores of the world. I won't leave.

The Man: You won't leave?

The Woman: That's my decision. Yes, I won't leave.

The Man: All right. *(Pause.)* Will you promise me you'll leave afterwards?

The Woman: As soon as you tell me why. Yes, I'll leave. *(A beat.)*

The Man: You promise?

The Woman: I promise. *(A beat.)*

The Man: All right. Come here.

THE WOMAN: No. You come over here.

THE MAN: You're afraid?

THE WOMAN: No. I already told you that.

THE MAN: So, come on over.

THE WOMAN: Up until now, I've been the one to come to you, the one who stood near you, over you, in order to talk to you. You sent me away. You want to talk to me. Now it's your turn to come to me.

THE MAN: You're the one who wants to know.

THE WOMAN: No. You're the one who's asking me to leave.

THE MAN: That's true.

THE WOMAN: So, come over here. *(He moves forward. Pause.)* Do you mind?

THE MAN: ...

THE WOMAN: Do you mind if I give you a compliment?

THE MAN: ...

THE WOMAN: You're a good-looking man.

THE MAN: ...

THE WOMAN: Very good-looking.

THE MAN: ...

THE WOMAN: That's all.

The Man: … *(He is facing her. They look at each other. A beat.)*

The Woman: I'm listening.

The Man: …

The Woman: Explain it to me.

The Man: …

The Woman: Explain your reasons to me.

The Man: …

The Woman: I'm listening.

(He violently slaps her. She falls on the ground, on her knees, at his feet.)

The Man: Did you understand?

The Woman: …

The Man: Did you understand?

The Woman: …

The Man: … Answer me.

The Woman: …

The Man: Answer me.

The Woman: …

The Man: You understood.

The Woman: …

The Man: I think you've understood.

The Woman: …

The Man: You can leave.

The Woman: …

The Man: You can leave.

The Woman: …

The Man: I'm going to take a swim. I'm going to do a few laps over there, far out in the ocean. When I come back, you'll be gone. You promised. You'll be gone.

The Woman: …

The Man: Have a good trip, miss.

The Woman: …

The Man; Have a good trip home.

(He goes into the ocean and quickly disappears. The Woman remains on her knees, on the ground. A beat. Her Friends arrive. They speak in low voices.)

The Female Friend: There she is. I hope there's still time. I hope it's not too late, that she hasn't met anyone. What got into me to let her come here? What got into me?

The Male Friend: Fuckin' heat, I'm telling you. Fuckin' heat.

The Female Friend: She's the one who insisted. She had just arrived. She was so happy, so pleased to see the shores again, the beach … I didn't have the heart to tell her the truth.

The Male Friend: This country's sick, I'm telling you. This country's sick.

The Female Friend: Look over there. Something's happened. Look over there. I should have told her, suggested some other beach, some other shore where I'd have explained everything to her, calmly.

The Male Friend: Fuckin' traffic jam, fuckin' traffic jam, fuckin' traffic jam, I'm telling you.

The Female Friend: She wouldn't have understood. She wanted her beach, like a stubborn child. She can't understand. She's not from here anymore. I don't see how I could explain to her that she doesn't have the right to come to the shores of the world anymore.

The Male Friend: Let me handle it. It won't take long. I'm going to talk to her. She'll listen to me and then we'll go. Let me handle it.

The Female Friend: Why? That's what she's going to ask you. Why? Why can't I have a picnic on my childhood beach? I'm curious to know how you're going to go about it.

The Male Friend: You're too curious. You'll see. End of discussion. You'll see.

The Female Friend: And if you answer her question, she'll have to accept that explanation. Are you ready to debate the pros and cons of five centuries of history, expose your arguments, develop them in detail? Are you ready to do that?

The Male Friend: I told you I'm in charge here. Let me handle it. I'm going to talk to your friend and then we'll get out of here.

The Female Friend: You don't know her. Her mind can't be changed. *(She doesn't budge.)* You'll have to convince her, persuade her, show her. I didn't have the strength to do that over the phone when she'd just arrived and was so happy and full of illusions. I didn't have the strength. The battle's lost before it's even begun. She won't understand. Nobody can understand that particular explanation if they're not from here. Nobody.

The Male Friend: You talk too much. Let me handle it.

(They move toward her.)

The Woman *(Stretched out flat on the ground)*: A man slapped me …

The Male Friend: Fuck, fuck, fuck. I'm sorry. I'm sorry we're late. Today's not my lucky day. The alarm didn't go off. We woke up late. You know how it is here. It's just drive to work, work all day, and go to bed. Same old, same old, all week long. From Monday to Saturday. Sunday's the day to snooze. So we slept in. We slept and slept and we overslept. Got up, had a fuckin' cuppa coffee, prepared this fuckin' picnic, more time wasted. Halfway here, unbelievably hot, we're dying of thirst and guess what? No bottle opener. Fuck! I can't believe it! Had to go back. Got the bottle opener and off we go again. This time it's a traffic jam: people coming from Mass, from baptisms, weddings, shit like that … Fuckin' crowds everywhere. You honk your horn, you're patient, you shout "Long live the bride!" like an asshole so you can finally get away from those fuckin' processions. I'm telling you. On the main highway, more fuckin' traffic: people coming from fishing trips, from the beach … Crowds, endless crowds. You can't move, no way, not one damn inch. Shit. You're dying from the heat, you're getting upset, you get into a fight, your car breaks down! A fuckin' breakdown, right in the middle of the highway, at noon, on a fuckin' Sunday! I lost my cool, I'm telling you, I lost my cool! I can't imagine how we got here. Shit! So, we're here, you're here, let's scram.

The Woman: A man slapped me …

THE FEMALE FRIEND: I was worried. I told him I shouldn't have let her leave by herself; he said you're a big girl, you'll know how to deal with the situation. I told him, the beaches are dangerous, people are attacked. He said the shore's a safe place, you'd be safe there, he said, you'd have nothing to be afraid of. I told him we're late, she's going to be all alone, lost, abandoned. He said what if it turns out you're late too, that you overslept, what with jet lag and being tired and all, that you'd be the last one to show up. It's my fault. Oh God, it's my fault …

THE WOMAN: A man slapped me …

THE MALE FRIEND: I told you she wouldn't get bored. People are assholes but they're nice. I told you not to worry, if she gets there ahead of us, she'll wait for us. You see? If she's alone, she'll go for a swim, she'll walk on the beach, up and down, for hours. Women love that. She'll enjoy digging for shells like when you were kids. Women love that. If another woman comes along, they'll hang out, they'll gab and swap stories about their lives. Women love that. If a guy comes along, she'll flirt with him, she'll charm him, she'll turn him on, then you won't be able to separate them. You see, no reason to worry. Good, let's scram.

THE WOMAN: A man slapped me …

THE FEMALE FRIEND: Yes, let's leave right away. I asked the old man in the straw hat to watch the car. He can't stay there forever. Let's go. We've got friends waiting for us on another beach. We'll introduce you. You'll see. That beach is a hundred times more beautiful than this one. It's a dream of a beach, with golden sand as far as the eye can see. They're waiting for us. There's a barbecue, spicy sausage, rum and music. It's a party, just for you. To celebrate your return home. To say welcome back and tell you how happy we are that you're back with us. Come. *(A beat.)*

THE WOMAN: A man slapped me. I got here. You weren't here. I was waiting for you. I saw him. He was over there, lying on the sand. I spoke to him. He answered me. He got up. He came over. He slapped me. He slapped me. *(A beat.)*

The Female Friend: Come on. Come with us. Let's go. We can't stay here. We'll be better off somewhere else, on another beach, sitting around with friends and you can tell us all about it. Come with us.

The Male Friend: Wait. Listen to her. Listen to what she has to say. It's super-serious. We can't let him get away with this. We can't let that happen. If she's telling the truth, we've got to go find that bastard.

The Woman: He slapped me. He was there, standing across from me, facing me, I could see his face in my eyes. He looked at me. I was smiling at him. He looked at me. He slapped me. Without any warning, as if it were natural, normal, as if it were inevitable. He slapped me.

The Female Friend: Let's not make any trouble. Let's get out of here. We haven't any right to be here. This isn't a public beach anymore. We're trespassing. We'll settle all that later, far away from here. Let's go.

The Male Friend: Wait. It's super-serious. It's an accusation. She says she was slapped. Who slapped her? Who was the bastard? Where is he? Where is that son of a bitch hiding? Do you see anyone? I don't see anybody. Where is he?

The Woman: He slapped me. Then he dove into the water and disappeared, over there, far away. He's in the water. That's where you have to go to find him and ask him why. Why he slapped me.

The Female Friend: Be reasonable. Get up. You'll feel better standing up. We're going to walk. We're going to go away from here and everything will be fine. You'll forget soon enough. Nothing happened. Come with us.

The Male Friend: In the water? He's in the water? I'm looking at the ocean. I'm looking at it as far as I can see. I don't see a thing, nobody, not a fuckin' thing. Ask her, ask your friend if she's sure about what's she saying.

The Woman: He slapped me. Touch me, here. That's a man's hand, a man's real hand, a hand that strikes out, that hits hard and that smacked me hard, right here, on this spot. Touch my face, here.

The Female Friend: I believe you. I take your word for it, but please let's go. There's nothing we can do if we stay here. It's illegal. If you want our help, let's leave this beach.

The Male Friend: Maybe your girlfriend's hallucinating. She fell asleep under this fuckin' sun and she dreamed up this whole crazy thing. The sun sometimes plays tricks on you. You wake up with your cheeks burning and you make up all kinds of stories. She's hallucinating, right? Bad sun, bad dreams, bad beach … A crappy day. Let's get out of here.

The Woman: He slapped me and I won't leave until I find out why. I want to know why. You know what I mean? I want to know. A stranger slapped me. I want to understand why. I want to understand why. *(A beat.)*

The Female Friend: Explain it to her.

The Male Friend: How?

The Female Friend: Explain it to her.

The Male Friend *(Pause)*: I can't.

The Female Friend: You promised.

The Male Friend: I can't.

The Female Friend: But you …

The Male Friend: Yes, I know I promised! I know I promised! But that was before, before I got to know your girlfriend. You can see it's not possible to discuss it, to explain anything. Not like this. Not in these conditions. She says a guy slapped her. OK. I accept that, but where is he, this guy? I ask you, where is he? She says he disappeared in the water. OK. I wonder, is he a guy or a sailor? If he's a sailor, where's his boat? Where is it? She says that he disappeared in the water. OK. I wonder is he a sailor or a shark? You gotta know. Listen, I'm happy to do whatever I can, I'm happy to be of service and help a poor lady in distress, but she's gonna have to get off the drugs. Because asking me to go out on the high seas to smash the face of a fish that smacked her one, that's making an ass out of me! A real ass! *(Pause.)* OK. Let's say she's telling the truth. Some guy smacked her one. So then the question is what did she do to him? I ask you, what did she do to him? I am a man. I know the men on this island. They have their faults but they never hit anyone for no reason. A man doesn't hit someone unless he's been backed up against a wall. What did she do? She has no right to be here. She must have insisted. She provoked him. She made fun of him. She tried his patience. She chatted him up, came on to him. The guys here don't like that. He came over. She pushed him away. He slapped her. You can understand that. She went too far. She doesn't know her place. She doesn't know her place. *(A beat.)*

The Female Friend: Explain it to her.

The Male Friend: …

The Female Friend: Explain to her why she's out of place here.

The Male Friend: …

The Female Friend: Tell her why she has no right to stay here, on this beach.

The Male Friend: …

The Female Friend: Neither one of us has the right.

The Male Friend: …

The Female Friend: Explain it to her.

The Male Friend: …

The Female Friend: Explain it to her.

The Male Friend *(A beat)*: I'm going on ahead. I'll wait for you in the car. *(He moves off.)* Fuckin' country.

(The two women are kneeling down, next to each other.)

The Woman: He hurt me, you know.

The Female Friend: I'm so sorry.

The Woman: Why? Why did he do that?

The Female Friend: I don't know.

The Woman: Why did he do that?

The Female Friend: I don't know. *(A beat.)*

The Woman: We're on the shores of the world.

The Female Friend: Right.

The Woman: It's the beach where we used to play when we were kids.

The Female Friend: Right.

The Woman: We were supposed to meet here.

The Female Friend: … *(A beat.)*

The Woman: That man, the one who hurt me, he says that I don't have any right to come here anymore.

The Female Friend: He told you that?

The Woman: Yes.

The Female Friend: He's right.

The Woman: You say that too. You're telling me I don't have the right to come here anymore.

The Female Friend: Yes, that's what I'm telling you. I don't have the right to come here anymore either. That's true.

The Woman: Explain that to me. *(A beat.)*

The Female Friend: Do you remember our childhood on this beach?

The Woman: Yes.

The Female Friend: How old were we?

The Woman: We were just children. *(A beat.)*

The Female Friend *(Digging in the sand)*: Do you remember the games we used to play in the sand?

The Woman: Sort of, yeah … there were so many of them …

The Female Friend: But the girl games in particular, on the beach, just between us, between girls, do you remember them?

The Woman: … *(A beat.)* … What are you doing?

The Female Friend: Help me.

The Woman: To do what?

The Female Friend: Help me. *(They dig in silence.)*

The Woman: What's that?

The Female Friend: The bathtub game. Remember?

The Woman: ... No ...

The Female Friend: You remember: you dig a hole, a basin, a tub, the biggest you can make.

The Woman: And then what?

The Female Friend: You stand up, one of us behind the other. Come over here. Come in front of me.

The Woman: And then what?

The Female Friend: We wait. *(A beat.)*

The Woman: Wait for what?

The Female Friend: Wait for the ocean. *(A beat.)*

The Woman: It won't come. It's low tide.

The Female Friend: Shush! Don't talk. Don't laugh. You have to wait until the ocean deigns to come to our basin. *(A beat.)* Don't you remember, we'd wait a long time. We could wait for hours for the ocean to come fill up our basin. A basin of white sand that ends up filled with sea water. Clear, white, pure water in the bottom of our bathtub, right under our feet. After that, we have to jump. Take off and jump. Jump over it so we don't fall into the bath. Don't you remember?

The Woman: ... I ... I don't ... I don't remember ...

THE FEMALE FRIEND: Jump with all your might. Jump as high as possible. Jump as far as possible, without falling. Above all, you mustn't fall. The one who falls, the one who's unfortunate enough to get one foot wet, the one who falls, loses the game. She's failed. She's eliminated from the game, from the group, from the beach. She disappears and no longer has the right to come play on the shores of the world. That's the punishment for having touched the bath water, contaminated it and made it dirty. Don't you remember?

THE WOMAN: I don't remember that.

THE FEMALE FRIEND: So jump then.

THE WOMAN: ...

THE FEMALE FRIEND: Jump.

THE WOMAN: ...

THE FEMALE FRIEND: Jump! You want to know why you can't stay on this beach? Jump and you'll find out. Jump! Jump! Jump! *(She pushes THE WOMAN. THE WOMAN resists.)*

THE WOMAN: I don't want to play! I don't want to jump! Stop! Stop and tell me the truth! Tell me the truth! *(A beat. Slowly, THE FEMALE FRIEND stands back, takes off, and jumps without much conviction. She falls into the hole.)* Where are you going?

THE FEMALE FRIEND: I'm leaving.

THE WOMAN: Don't leave. Wait.

THE FEMALE FRIEND: I lost. I have to leave.

THE WOMAN: Don't leave me all alone. Wait.

The Female Friend: I can't stay. You have to respect the rules of the game. I have to leave.

The Woman: Look! He's coming back. It's that man! That man! He's coming back! Stay with me!

The Female Friend: Come with me. Don't stay there. You're out of place here. Come on.

The Woman: I can't go. I can't. I have to know. I have to know. Stay with me.

The Female Friend: You have to know your place. Your rightful place. You know where to find me …

(She's gone. The Woman hesitates, then decides to wait. A beat. The Man comes out of the water. He takes his beach towel. He dries himself. The Woman goes over to him.)

The Woman: You hit me, sir.

The Man: …

The Woman: You hit me, sir.

The Man: …

The Woman: I'm speaking to you. *(The Man stops drying himself. He doesn't move.)* You hit me.

The Man: …

The Woman: Why, sir, did you hit me?

The Man: …

The Woman: Why did you hit me?

The Man: …

The Woman: Why?

The Man: …

The Woman: Why?

The Man: Get out of here.

The Woman: You know very well that I can't leave now. It's no longer possible. You know that. For mysterious reasons, you chased me away from your beach and for some other reasons that are even more mysterious, you forced me to stay when you hit me. Explain that to me, sir.

The Man: No, miss, you're the one who owes me an explanation. There are hundreds of beaches on this island; beaches, shores, and bays with unobstructed views; coves full of fish and creeks with lagoons. Hundreds of them. And you chose mine, deliberately. What are you looking for?

The Woman: I already told you: meet up with my friends, here, my childhood … I wanted to get here by myself, I got lost, I got here late. My friends have just left. They can vouch for me.

The Man: You're lying. You don't have any friends. They can't be here. They can't live here like you said they do. Everybody who lives on this island knows in no uncertain terms that this beach, that used to be called the shores of the world, is private, reserved, inaccessible. So tell me why.

The Woman: I don't have any other reasons except the ones I told you. I'm on vacation, I came back to my native country. I came to recharge my batteries, to relax and get some rest away from big city violence, away from the noise, honking cars, and pollution. I was fed up with all that. I came to see something different.

The Man: You're lying. If you're from here, you'd know that violence has never left these shores. It's gotten worse: the same traffic jams, the same noisy cars, the same shifty looks from dogs and people on the streets and the blazing sun beating down on us. The sun that gets a hard-on, darts its rays at us, wearing us down more every day and driving us to do things that don't work out.

The Woman: That's too easy. It's not the sun's fault. I think the sun's just fine. It's warm, just right and certainly not hostile. You're the one with the problem. You attacked me. You think I've got hidden intentions when I'm telling you the truth. I'm telling you the truth.

The Man: You're lying. You don't know it yet but you're lying. You're giving me apparent reasons, fallacious reasons, transparent reasons, for your being here, on my shores. I heard them. I don't believe you. I ask you to look inside yourself and tell me why my beach and no other one. Look inside and answer me.

The Woman: I'm not looking for anything. If you knew me, you'd know that I'm a simple, uncomplicated woman. I lead the normal life of an average city person who's had enough of jackhammers. I'm a happy, healthy person and you're wrong to think I have hidden intentions. I'm not looking for anything.

The Man: You're lying. We're all looking for something. All of us. You don't know it yet but you're looking. Even if you don't know it. You chose a forbidden beach with impunity knowing full well you might be struck. And you're staying on, you're hanging on, you don't want to leave until you've found what you don't know you're looking for. That's not innocent.

The Woman: I refuse to follow you in your faulty reasoning. You're not the victim. You're not the person who's been insulted. You're not the one who, right this very minute, is still feeling the sting from your slap, the humiliation and the helplessness. You're hardly in a position to demand an apology, justice, or an explanation.

The Man: Nevertheless, I am asking for one. I'm even demanding one. Your insolence irritated me. Your stubbornness provoked me. Your disobedience forced me to punish you. Yes, I really mean forced. You're looking for something and I have every right to know what that is.

The Woman: You're changing the subject, sir. You're getting off track. You're changing the subject to make me believe that I'm in the wrong when I'm asking for the truth. You say that I'm necessarily looking for something. I'll give you that. What I'm looking to understand, is the how and the why. How a man reaches a point where he'll hit a woman and why you blame me. That's what I'm looking for, sir, and I'm convinced that you can give me an answer.

The Man: I blame you for your lack of courtesy. You walked onto my beach without being announced, without knocking, without ringing the bell, with your shoes on your feet and with the step of a conqueror. You weren't concerned about whether or not I was sleeping, dreaming, or how my tan was coming along. No, you rolled right in as if you had conquered this terrain and you didn't even say hello.

The Woman: A beach is an open space, free of charge, free and accessible to everyone. That's what people say about all the beaches, all the shores throughout the world. I couldn't have known. I didn't say hello. I don't remember that.

The Man: I blame you for being too formal with me. Like a stranger. By doing that, you kept me at a distance as if you were letting me know that you aren't from here anymore, that you're just passing through, and that there are oceans between us. I recognized you. You're a stranger.

The Woman: But I don't know you. It was the least I could do. I couldn't be familiar with you. You should have told me you were uncomfortable with that. You could have just asked me to be more informal. You don't make any sense, sir. You don't make any sense.

The Man: I blame you for not knowing how to behave, how to show restraint. You thought it was enough to ask and you would receive, to knock and the door would open. That's not true. Not on this beach. You don't have the knack or the manner. Especially a certain way of being. You don't have the necessary reserve. Your look is haughty, arrogant, and disrespectful. You didn't show me any respect when you took me for one of those tight-assed men whose services older women procure on the shores of our world.

The Woman: You're over-sensitive. I gave you compliments like people do to be pleasant, sociable and to pass the time. It didn't mean anything. You're not my type. You're not my size. I don't find you attractive.

The Man: You're a foreigner. Like the ones we see getting off the ships every year at the same time, in the same season, for two or three weeks of vacation. You have their counterfeit manners, an unsure way of walking, clothes that are too big and perfume that's overbearing.

The Woman: I'm not a foreigner.

The Man: I'm not talking about legitimate foreigners who aren't from here, who don't speak our language, and who naively come here to burn their flesh to a crisp under the sun of our trade winds.

The Woman: I'm not a foreigner.

The Man: I'm not talking about those fat milk cow foreigners, the ones who sweat from the heat under their madras-colored parasols.

The Woman: I'm not a foreigner.

The Man: No, I'm not talking about those typical foreign women who arrogantly strut about on our made-for-tourist beaches. They aren't from here and in their barb-wired hotels they give them maps so they won't get lost on the forbidden shores. The hospitality we owe them doesn't commit us to anything. It's not real. It's expected and they know how to be satisfied with it. They don't stick around when we've made it clear they aren't welcome. They don't insist because their opinion of us is already formed. They aren't from here.

THE WOMAN: But I've told you that I'm not a foreigner.

THE MAN: I'm talking about you, the foreign women who were born on the shores of this world and who abandoned them for gray skies and citadels. I'm talking about you who are no longer from here or from any place else and who have forgotten who you are and where you came from. You come back to the shores of your childhood, for a little stroll or a picnic, like some profane pilgrimage. You've forgotten that we are on an island of social strata, ranks and casts and that we're not all equal under the sun. That it's not enough for both of us to get undressed, on a particular beach, to make us the same or to make us similar. We're not from the same shores. You've forgotten that.

THE WOMAN: ...

THE MAN: Do you want to know why this beach is forbidden to you?

THE WOMAN: ...

THE MAN: Do you really want to know that?

THE WOMAN: ...

THE MAN: I'm going to tell you.

THE WOMAN: ...

THE MAN: You don't have the right color skin. It isn't appropriate. It isn't according to the rules. It isn't allowed to wander freely around the shores of the world. The color of your skin, miss, makes a stain on my shores and neither you nor anyone of the same range of colors are authorized to cross over them, to tramp on them, to stride over them. That's how it is and everyone on this fucking island knows that. And your friends, if they really exist, would have told you that and repeated it like God-given orders that can't be disobeyed. That's the way it is. It's our legacy. It's the destiny of this God-forsaken people who chose to live in a land enclosed by the color of their skin. I can't do anything about it. Your skin doesn't belong here. It doesn't fit. It carries with it memories that don't belong here, in my domain. I can't do anything about it. Your skin is not the right color. *(THE MAN goes back to his towel. A beat. Long silence.)* You aren't devastated.

THE WOMAN: ...

THE MAN: You aren't devastated.

THE WOMAN: ...

THE MAN: You knew all that.

THE WOMAN: ...

THE MAN: You knew it, didn't you?

THE WOMAN: ...

THE MAN: You knew it all along.

THE WOMAN: ...

THE MAN: I thought so.

THE WOMAN: ...

THE MAN: I thought so all along.

THE WOMAN: ...

The Man: You never did question my property rights. Maybe I lied. Maybe this beach is not what I told you it was. I hit you. You should have protested. You should have sued me, rebelled. You didn't do any of that because you knew. You knew who I was, my family's power on this island and what the color of my skin represents. You knew that it's useless to attack me, here on my shores. You took me at my word because you knew, through your friends, through rumor or instinctively, that this beach is off-limits to you. You knew that.

The Woman: Yes, I knew it. I've always known it. In my hazy childhood memories, I see a dark beach, crowded with people where we swam according to color, where we laughed according to color, where we played according to color, spread out on our multicolored beach towels. But it was a game. You had to keep your place, you had to obey your parents who'd say to you: don't go near them, don't bother them, don't mix with them. And we children of the shores enjoyed disobeying them. We'd escape into the dunes. We'd invent a thousand tricks in order to hide and touch each other and fool around, stifling our laughter at the foot of the rainbow. After that, we'd have to come back as if nothing had happened and confront our parents' knowing looks, for they weren't fooled and they pretended to disapprove. It was a game. And then we'd leave. We'd go to our separate homes, each one of us with his color correctly put away in an orderly fashion, and everybody was happy with that, and truth to tell, nobody took offense. Since there had to be a rule to play the game, why not that one? It was simple, clear, visible: you mustn't mix with the others. It was just a game. We children knew that, and we weren't worried because we also knew that a game can turn into something else, that rules change, and like opposites, colors are attracted to each other. They meet and mix. It's inevitable. It's mathematical and that's what happened. As a result of our fooling around with each other in the wet dunes, we changed the shores of this world. All you have to do is walk along the beaches to see it's true. There aren't any more colors. There are only men, women, and children with long hair or straight hair, with white teeth, bursts of laughter, a melodic tongue, and the sun who's the only one to decide what color the skin will be. There are no more colors.

THE MAN: When I told you that the sun is a capricious master, you didn't believe me. It mixes the colors, yes. It puts them through the fire of its desire, and apparently, it tans bodies and unifies skin tones and you might think that the miracle has been accomplished when you come to this island, that a new Babel is born, splendid and harmonious, without any differences, without prejudices, without distinction. But the sun has failed. The sun hasn't touched our hearts and our guts. It hasn't reached them. It has stayed on the surface. So that even if the skin tones have become unified, the order your parents gave you long ago has resurfaced and it's stronger, more radical, more definitive than ever. We cannot mix. That was a dangerous game. You played it but you underestimated the power of words and how they were emphasized. The words said that it was our story. What they meant was that you could not avoid that truth. You didn't listen. You coupled off. You merged, and in the sun's shade, you thought you could cover your tracks. You can't escape your past. The differences are there, in the hearts and in the guts and all we need is just one look to recognize the degree of color and its rightful place on the shores of the world. Just one look, and anybody who lives on this island can tell you your social status, your position, what line you mustn't cross and how far you can go. That's our gift, a kind of island genius. Color exists and if you don't believe me, ask the ocean: it'll tell you the incalculable number of skin colors that fade in its salty waters every day. The foam and the waves are witnesses to this. That's how it is. Come down from your skyscraper, come back to earth, your earth which hasn't changed. Oh no, it hasn't changed.

THE WOMAN: I want to believe it has changed. You're a young fool who is isolated on your beach and you can't see that thoughts mix together like the rest of the world. It's inevitable. It's an unstoppable movement, in people's minds and bodies. Get out, meet people, talk to them, exchange ideas and you'll see that I'm right. I'm not asking you to cross the ocean. Come with me, just over here, on the beach next to this one and I challenge you to find basic colors there. They don't exist. Not on the bodies, not in the hearts. But since you seem so sure of yourself and your talent, tell me: tell me what my color is.

The Man: Don't play games with me. Not that game. You're an agitator, a provocateur and you've come to find me, fully aware of what you're doing, to shake me up, drawn here by that prohibition of which you were well aware; a bit like those militant demonstrators who tie themselves to the bars of fences so that they'll be beaten up. You've got your battle wrong. We don't rebel here. There is no revolution, no emancipation. We go from one servitude to another, our backs bent over, more than happy to be on welfare. Here we are given a color and we take it for granted. The slap you received was the size of your color.

The Woman: Tell me what my color is.

The Man: Don't go looking for trouble.

The Woman: Tell me what my color is.

The Man: Don't go looking for trouble.

The Woman: Tell me what my color is.

The Man: …

The Woman: Tell me, sir. What color deserves a slap? What past history allows you to be and continue to be so violent with me? Tell me what memory, what pain, what suffering I bear despite myself that condemns me in your eyes? Can one be cursed in one's own land? I thought I was from here and that this island like the world completely belonged to me. That's what I thought. If that's not true, tell me what I have to do to know who I am. What boat must I take to find the shores of my childhood? I admit I'm afraid of the crossing and the bad storms at night, of being tossed about between the ocean and the sky. I'm afraid of sea sickness and the dawn's vomit. Will there be somebody there to keep the boat from sinking? Who will know how to initiate me into the rites of return? I have lost the memory of that. How many prayers must I say when I see the lights of the ancestral city far away? How many times must I kiss the sand, on my knees, how many times on the highways or the turnpike? How many tears, how much blood, how much absinthe in order to beg for pardon? Who? For what? I've lost the memory. Tell me, sir, tell me. *(A beat.)*

THE MAN: Since a slap is not enough to make you understand who you are and where you come from, I'm going to come over to you and we're going to have a fight. I propose an extremely violent fight between you and me. I'll be the attacker and you'll be the one attacked.

THE WOMAN: You ... You're crazy ... I'm not going to fight with you ... You're crazy ...

THE MAN: Yes, you are, you're going to fight. It will be rough, primitive, brutal. I'm going to attack you physically, with my considerable male strength and with my unstoppable desire. We're going to grab each other by the waist and I'm going to tear your clothes off, one piece at a time, tear them off like a laceration.

THE WOMAN: You're crazy ... I'm going to shout ... I'll scream ... I ...

THE MAN: You won't shout. You won't scream. You're going to struggle. With conviction, energetically, with all your female strength which is not much, but you'll do it in silence. We'll be fighting hand to hand, claw to claw, our eyes fixed on each other's eyes, and you will read in the corner of my eyes, the pleasure of the dominator and I'll read in the tragedy of your look, the panic of the dominated.

THE WOMAN: Stay back ... sir ... stay back.

THE MAN: I am going to beat you up. It will be serious and as it should be. I'll smash your face with my fists and hit you so hard in the stomach with my feet that you'll fall on the ground and lie there with your head buried in the sand. I'm going to hold your head down in the sand, bury it until you can't breathe and then from behind, yes, from behind, with your arms out in the form of a cross, your thighs spread, I am going to penetrate you.

The Woman: Don't come near me … don't come near me …

The Man: I'm going to penetrate you, dry, without preparation. It will be radical. It will take a long time. It will be painful and it will hurt. It will last as much time as you've made me waste here, since your arrival. As much time as you've been here on this beach, enough time for you to become aware. My penis will hurt but I'll keep on going, industriously, without caring about you, about your privacy, your breathing, without caring if you are still alive.

The Woman: Help … Help me … Help …

The Man: It will be pure, selfish, solitary, without generosity, and without an orgasm. And because you made me waste my time perspiring in vain, I'm going to beat you up again in order to have some pleasure at last. Then and only then will I be able to spit on you.

The Woman: Don't do that, sir … Have pity … Don't do that …

The Man: When I've finished, I'll stretch out and you'll be at my side, on our beach, like a young virgin on her bed of blood. We'll be here, the two of us, reconciled, reunited, sharing my crime, with your identity found at last, on the shores, on the shores of the world. After that, you can leave.

(He grabs her. A brief scuffle. She gets away. She slaps him, violently. He falls on the ground, on his knees.)

The Woman: Don't touch me.

The Man: …

The Woman: Don't touch me.

The Man: …

The Woman: It's alright.

The Man: …

The Woman: I understand.

The Man: …

The Woman: I understand.

The Man: …

The Woman: Thank you, sir.

The Man: …

The Woman: Now I know.

The Man: …

The Woman: I know.

The Man: …

The Woman: Thank you.

The Man: …

The Woman: I'm leaving.

The Man: …

The Woman: I'm leaving. *(Starts to go.)*

The Man: You hit me …

The Woman: …

The Man: You hit me …

The Woman: …

The Man: No one has ever hit me before …

The Woman: …

The Man: Do you hear me, no one …

The Woman: …

The Man: Especially not a woman …

The Woman: …

The Man: Not a woman … like you … *(The Woman starts to walk away again.)* Wait …

The Woman: …

The Man: Don't leave … Not right away … Wait …

The Woman: …

The Man: I wanted to tell you … You hit me … You hit me and I felt …

The Woman: …

The Man: I felt … desire …

The Woman: …

The Man: For the first time … the very first time …

THE WOMAN: ...

THE MAN: I'd like ... I'd like us to talk about it ...

THE WOMAN: ...

THE MAN: I'd like to understand ... Why, lost in violence ... with a forbidden woman ... a woman like you? What does that mean? ... Maybe you know? ... Maybe there is some other solution ... for colors and men ... something other than separation?

THE WOMAN: ...

THE MAN: Maybe you were right. Maybe we have to knock up against each other ... rub against each other ... collide with one another ... to learn how to know each other and try, yes try to forget the compartmentalization, our parents' voices that rule our dreams and spirit ... I don't know ... I don't know ...

THE WOMAN: ...

THE MAN: I'm confused ... I feel desire for you and I don't understand ... I'm confused ... Would you please stay so we can talk about it? Make yourself at home, sit down, take off your clothes so you can take a swim. Would you like that?

THE WOMAN: No. I didn't come here for that. I came from quite a distance to spend my vacation, a simple vacation, at the seashore, in my native country. This was where I was supposed to meet my friends for a picnic, here on this beach. Childhood friends. I wasn't looking for anything. I didn't want anything. I wasn't asking for anything. I was on vacation. But you have convinced me. There's no solution in the matter of color on these shores. Men, women live with this situation quite well. There's no way out, no solution, no hope that the two of us will be able to sit down calmly, some day on the shores of the world. That's the way it is. *(She leaves. THE MAN stays there, kneeling on the sand.)*

A.W.O.L.

Olivier Cadiot

Translated from the French novel Le Colonel des Zouaves
by Cole Swensen

Adapted for the stage by Marion Schoevaert

Wake up early.
Rent a fast car.
Turn into the drive between the open gates.
Floor it 7400 rpm's.
Several miles into the dark tunnel of overhanging trees.
Break out of the trees. Emerge in full light.
Double clutch. Slight skid around in a 146 degree arc. No tracks left in the plush gravel.
Cut the engine.
Leap over the low door, legs first followed by the head levered by the arms. Zip. Twist of the hips, and land both feet on the ground.

Double clutch. Slight skid around in a 146 degree arc. No tracks left in the plush gravel. Cut the engine. The Unknown Guest leaps gracefully over the car door and breaks his ankle.

Coming apart at the seams! Ha ha. Let's have a look at it.

Ripping open the trouser leg. *(Silent scream.) (CHORUS screams.)*

Now don't scream like that, it's not all that bad. We'll find you some decent camouflage for dinner.

Confused/shameful/ridiculous/sorry/my/my/leg/trou/trousers too tight/crack/idiot/sorry about the trouble/broken?

No no, it would hurt much more if it was broken, it's nothing. Let me see it. The foot is pretty bad. How does that feel there?

Scream. *(Silent scream.)* *(CHORUS screams.)*

Dressing room. Find slacks and matching jacket more or less the size of the wounded, who, at a glance, is 42-16-22.

There are a certain number of principles to be maintained under any and all circumstances, such as: Number 1: Unity and Economy—"The objective of the dish must satisfy a common taste." Number 2: Sacrifice—"Learn to repress strokes of pure aesthetic genius in favor of greater efficiency." Number 3: Serenity—"When in doubt, choose the moderate route."

You're limp as a dead fish, my boy. You've got to get it into gear. This isn't a retiring home. Do yourself a favor and get that straight right now if you want the kind of privileges that the others have already earned through years of good and loyal services.

These days, you've got to change your attitude, *work not only more but better*. It's the work itself that's changed. No more Yesssir, got a job and hop! Into a hammock for the rest of your life. Total service, think way beyond the task at hand. Which is to say do not stand around waiting for a thank you, get it?

Bell ring.

Emergency!

Get this suit downstairs on the double dring-dring hurry up tuck those elbows in let's go chop-chop dring-dring chop-chop.

The Unknown Guest opens the car door and gets out in a dignified fashion.

Before replying to my respectful salutations with a dull half-cough, he cocks his finger toward the luggage in the trunk, pivots on his heel

and turns his back on me to admire the view. Light late-afternoon mist. 18:45; 105 minutes to dinner.
Nothing happens. At ease. It'll be all right, breathing normal, nothing unusual has occurred. He has not broken his ankle.
There are no tire tracks in the gravel.
All is well.
Both arms hang at rest, hands relaxed, breathe. Breathe, stretch, breathe. Flex. Eyes on the horizon, exhale. Calm.

Bring me a drink!

Conversion: 180 degrees; open hidden service door. Got to wake up instantly. Try too hard, slows you down. Ultra-rapid descent of emergency spiral staircase, arrival at office: 23.1 seconds, I am out of shape.
Just not up to speed.
A good pound of very dry ice cubes into shaker, splash of vermouth. Filtered once, triple measure of gin + extra dash, filter again. Pour. Place glass on tray. Move out, think nothing, head clear, look straight at enormous snowflakes besieging the Assyrian windows of the corner salon.
Half-turn to the right. Right. Stop, present tray. Tray.

(Chorus stands up.)

United we stand.

Ah … chaa!
God bless you!

Hitler used to say:
we're a country of small farmers who could lead
the fashion industry.
You know he's not entirely wrong,
though a few things have changed.
But not all that much, eh?

We'd all be Bolshevik-farm whores or (...)
gentlemen-farmer-collectors?
That's exactly what I mean.
It's precisely that.
That's just how I see it.
I see it just like you do (...) .
It's great to think that you share your neighbor's
opinions,
you say to yourself I am not wrong after all,
it's an extraordinary sensation and
—how can I put it—personally,
Ahhhhh *(Yawning.)*
Tcha!
God bless you!

CHORUS:
The class struggle
is just lip service we all know it's every man for
himself

All right then it does no good
to try and help a guy out
It's just like in the pogroms
you tell them to split
They stay
Why? Held back by purely
material
considerations

I am at the center of the living
room.
Eavesdropping, slows
you down. Control hold
finger on tray. Red carpet crossing.
March straight,
stare with dignity follow the
imaginary line from a
point on the wall to the central
window obscured by
snow.
I conquer yard after yard of red
Persian carpet.
And the microscopic birds hiding
behind those

no doubt

It's crazy this notion

that the common people have an opinion
where does this come from?

We know it only too well

It's a new idea there's "soul everywhere"
You might as well let the ducks and chickens vote
What the hell are you doing?

enormous leaves, how are they doing?
I'd be in there with them. Doing well. I am there
and I'm staying. It's the life I've dreamed of. I curl
around the branches like an acrobat on his trapeze.
Like only I know how.
In nature's reserve for a moment, unlisted in the
census. I've got appropriate feathers; in a minute,
I'll be whistling "Ooh, ooh, I'm Rob." I'm going to
whistle … don't … don't … oh no … I'm
whistling.

I am stretched out in the pattern of the central carpet, red and green labyrinth. If you plaster your eye right up against it, you can follow it. A myopic promenade at the level of dust. I'm a crumb in the hedges of green wool, my name is Thing, Mr. Whatzit, Rob, Whatnot, I'm swallowed up in the paths of paradise.

I hear nothing. I'm a crumb in the hedges of green wool, my name is Thing. Turn left. I'm a crumb in the hedges of green wool, my name is Thing. Turn right. I'm a crumb in the hedges of green wool; my name is Thing.

What the hell are you doing with your mouth all puckered up like a chicken's ass?

What are you doing?

Very slowly I realize that this question is being addressed to me. Already far away, lost in the paths of red and green fibers, having almost reached the central paradise without having once gone over the line, hopping on one foot. I'm a crumb in the hedges of green wool, my name is Thing. I'm a crumb in the hedges of green wool, my name is Thing. Blind among all these fronds, I sweep up the non-existent ash and leave.

(Singing.) O my oh so lovely Valentine oof oof / oof oof, I run in the woods of blue cedar/ the twigs snap under the iron of my boots / My name is John Robinson / I am the field runner / My name is John Robinson, son of Rob / I descend the mountains / The son of the red-breasted robin / Oof oof.

Robinson that's me.

I crawl across the field in silence, nose in the grass. My shadow looms dangerously over the water, so I decide to become smaller as only I know how. The landscape becomes larger.

Sounds grow. Rolling of pebbles + sound of foam.

Everything shifts, the grasses are trees, the banks are cliffs, the verges are forests. Fish align themselves like bombers in the sky.

Everything is in everything.

That's how I see it.

It's beautiful.

I hold the light foam still persistent in the dark with a question in my mind occupying more and more space available for thoughts. The still persistent in the dark clarity of the foam. The in the dark still persistent clarity of the foam. Question.

The more and more pressing question.

The question: What happens to fish in the dark? And I fall asleep in the grass.

With infinite precaution I follow the curve of the lacquered wall along the great corridor as I carry the platter. Three hundred yards, murmur of voices growing as I approach the dining room. Two hundred yards, slight inclination of platter to compensate for curve. One hundred yards. Sixty degree curve in front of the consoles, clicking of tongue, opening door. I enter, lights up, exclamations.

It's so beeauuuutiful ahhhhhh! So beautiful. What a fish!
From around here? Just in front? From that ditch? From those black ponds?

From the lake! Bang, battle!

I put on my 180 degree eye vision, squinting in order to memorize the blurred faces of the guests, comparing the shadows with the names memorized from the seating plan.
Two brief breaths. Twitch of the nose out of superstition I will dispel bad memories.
Kick-turn, approach table.
Platter direction left toward female-guest number one pause two inches from her fingers, with a gentle swing that coordinates the arm and the shoulder placing the body's weight forward. Finish off the gesture with an invisible shift of the wrist, suggest that she serve herself the brochet.
I could not possibly drop the platter, I will not drop the platter, these are my two hands holding the platter, no problem. I have been in service since time began.
A slight nod of the head toward my assistant like that a pianist makes to the page-turner, send the sauce. Adds a human touch to the choreography. Take two steps back, freeze. At ease.

Chorus:
Who pays the bill who pays for welfare?
Idea, sure, like maid's ideas "Mister, Mister I've got an idea!" God help us!
Atchaa!
God bless you!
Atchaa!

God help us
Atchaa!
God bless you! *(Continues over speech of* BUTLER.*)*

I can't listen to everything, I serve. I pay attention to what I do. I will dispel bad memories. I hum in order to forget that there's something I must forget. I'm very experienced, I've got an iron will, I am simply impeccable, I will not drop that platter.

Pure work no friction.

I am in perfect control.

I am here, that's me, those are my hands holding the platter, there's no problem, I see the platter, I very softly hum the song that allows me to do things in real time.

I am I and no one else.

I will not drop that platter. Three more people to serve, no one hears my song. I sing very softly behind my teeth, I smile microscopically, I am a machine error free guaranteed, I'm flexible and coordinated, I am still life.

I retreat trusting the rest of the service to my assistants. One hundred percent success.

Mission accomplished.

With the exception of that disagreeable moment when M said to the person at the end of the table: Stop, er kann verstehen.

He-he-he is [] he has [] he showed a-a-a [] his [] said the redheaded girl.

As if I was doing something unusual. Stop, er kann verstehen.

Effectively conveying by this gesture that number one I was precisely what he didn't want said and that I had "misbehaved." That number two I couldn't decipher this language code. And that number three I will continue to become more and more that which should not be said. Till the end of time.

The "Stop" sounded like a Shhh! and all I heard of the rest was something like "kannverstehen." The name of a Dutch knight? A magic formula to dispel an evil thought? Shhh kannverstehen!

I know perfectly well how to make covering remarks in a duck voice, as the situation sometimes requires.

Chorus:

Hitler used to say: we're a country of small	Quack-quack-quack
farmers who could lead the fashion industry.	Quack-quack-quack
You know he's not entirely wrong, though a few	Quack-quack-quack
things have changed. But not all that much, eh?	Quack-quack-quack
	Quack-quack-quack

Ten o'clock, sir. Tray in hand, mail sorted, newspaper ironed.

Instantly unfold tray table. Remove metal dome from plate. Omelet à la menthe, sausage #3, smoked breast, braised tomatoes, green beans in juice of mutton, toast.

Open paper.

There must be a way to avoid the use of the third person which slows you down. If it would please Monsieur, etc.

Use a different approach. Don't say: If Monsieur would like to take a look at page four, where there's a picture of the scene of the crime that so intrigues Monsieur. Say: look at on which it is of the scene of the that so intrigues crime *Page four*.

The important word at the end, that way people listen to you and don't cut you off.

And here's boiled but not too long served on toast lightly spread with parsley butter Eggs.

Breakfast is served.

I glance over his shoulder, to get a look at page four. Photo of a family all lined up. How strange, if I'd murdered them, I wouldn't have buried them in front of my own door. Man Buries Own Family Under Front Lawn. Huge headline four columns wide.

There's something fishy here sir.

Give me a break, would you? Not in the morning. How many times do I have to tell you: Not in the morning. Which language should I use?

Would Monsieur like me to trim his mustache?

Tomorrow.

Close eyes retrace corridor toward room. File images of burial mounds in memory folder. Label it "Crime" to avoid misplacing.
It's mine.

(Throws a stone into the guest's direction.) They raise their heads and look, but see nothing back there where I am not. Actually, listening is best up in the trees. Out there on the end of a branch, it's like being right at the tip of an antenna. The perfect post for deciphering voices rising up between the leaves.
Spy cap, no one's going to spot me. Oh good.

CHORUS:

Yes, yes, yes, yes, yes, yes, yes. Yes, yes, yes, yes, yes, yes, yes.

If you observe a beehive very carefully, if you're a fan of the habitat as I am, you see of course that the Queen Mother Bee gets screwed by the same male several times, which means that in addition to having a whole slew of half-sisters, they have a certain number of super-sisters in common, with whom they share rich chromosomal affinities.

Fasch-in-a-ting

Yes, yes, yes, yes, yes, yes, yes. Yes, yes, yes, yes, yes, yes, yes.

We need a governmental decree to extract a priori
this mental gangrene

If a citizen has a rotten limb
you cut it off no time to stand around and talk about it

And if there's no more ether Major
you go ahead with it anyway

Bite down on that my boy
you stick a bit between his teeth
and off you go.

We've got to do something
I'm not talking about bringing in the army
no need to go that far
just a little turn of the screw eh?
United we sit.

(CHORUS sits.)

The old traditions of our profession, they're over, done, gone.

Gentlemen, service has changed. The very concept has changed.
The very concept. Why?

Dead silence.

Because conditions have changed. They've forgotten. Moral we've got to add in little extras to let them know that the work is being done to perfection.
If you are serving rabbit "à la royale" put a little crown on its head so they can get the point.
Today's topic: "Crumbing."
Two techniques?

The scraper and the the the—the little thing you roll across the table that has the little crumb-catcher underneath.

A crumber! Take thumb/index, control with ring finger, arm-wrist-hand become a single unit, that's the secret. Always pull toward the crumb, from in front to behind, never push the crumb. Risk of sending it flying. Add a subtle shift of the hip, small, discrete, just enough to give a bit of rhythm to the act, like that, see? To add a little style, no?

Yes.

NO, to drive the crumber toward the objective while avoiding skidding it all over the table. Gains time and creates subconscious sense of security in the dinner, total service, admiration that reflects upon our master, and therefore upon us.

And therefore upon us.

Good, good-good-good. Conclusion: we must know everything about the client, down to the last button. Tendencies, desires, potential for modification of tastes. The curve of needs and wants.
Cough. Sit back. And into the abounding silence, I list the subjects to be covered next time. Pause. Then slowly raise my eyes and drop a condescending, "You are dismissed."

(Singing.) If my aunt had had some / She would have been my uncle.
If my aunt had had some / She would have been my uncle.

In every calculation, there's a margin of error. You've got to reduce that error to the point of chance. When a guy tells you I wanted this like that, there's been some mistake, I wanted tea not coffee, you can be sure that he's already in the enemy camp.
Today, you have to think upstream of the situation. You could say that things that haven't been invented haven't been invented because they're not needed. Right?

Right.

NO. Novelty is always needed.

No-vel-teee.

Example, suppose I've planned a rabbit for lunch. It must be raised on seasonal wild grasses in a clean hutch. Why?

Because it's cleaner.

NO. To improve the race. By raising them in maximum hygiene, progress is made. By selective breeding, you can get blind rabbits that think of nothing but eating. Which is how we came up with the idea of Basement Hutches.

What do you do when the rabbit is dead?

Silence.

First, skin it, beginning with a cut between the back feet. Then insert your hand to enlarge the opening. Break the bone of the thigh above the knee. Cut off the feet. Pass the feet out through the hole made at the beginning. Dislocate the upper thighs and turn back the skin by pulling it toward the head to finish the job.

Another example. Come up here George. Stand there. Very good.

"George Brings M's Newspaper."

We're going to play that scene. You are George, naturally and I am M. Off we go. Go on George.

This world we live in there's something, what's the word, atrocious about it don't you think? If Monsieur will permit me to say so. Death on every page.

Very good. Typical response from M: What the hell are you babbling on about George?

Or, atrocious why do you say atrocious, George? That's just life.

In both cases, George must come back with "Atrocious Sir." It's tough to do that "Atrocious Sir." Let me hear you say it with a truly somber voice. Go on.

Atrocious Sir this pervasive suffering.

Very good. Go on. Do the whole thing.

This World we live in there's something, what's the word, atrocious about it don't you think? If Monsieur will permit me to say so. Death on every page.

Excellent. That's the Art of Household Organization. It's the latest technique. Maximum care-taking production, faithful adherence to Dr. Be-good-to-yourself-this-morning. Good luck gentlemen.
Off we go. Last exercise, exit the room gracefully with a plate on your head and your two
hands tied behind your back. While hopping. Just kidding. Ah ah ah.

What if someone saw me? All alone in front of a small puddle. Just sitting here, 950 out, hair a mess, wearing a dark heavy suit, half lost in the grass, what must I look like?
But they can't see me, I've dug a trench. It's practically a house, with a wooden center pole, piles of cushions, gas lamp, tartan covers, tuna fish sandwiches, hard-boiled eggs, etc. All the books neatly arranged in a bookcase, and, if they are too long, a hand-written summary of their story.

1. For instance, one guy talks about his childhood and at one point, because of piece of cake he drags through his tea, he suddenly remembers his entire past, perfectly intact, not reduced to a single phrase, like it'll be when you're dying, but in real time. So you find yourself dealing with someone who's saying very slowly that he's telling you his memories really fast. Or vice-versa.
2. One morning, a man finds himself transformed into a cockroach or a giant rabbit. Naturally, his family is horrified. He doesn't come out of his room much anymore. Things seem to be getting worse, etc.
3. A man decides to leave his native country and is shipwrecked. As soon as he's established the minimal conditions for existence, he launches into more and more elaborate and unnecessary projects until he becomes a saint without knowing it.

I am at the bottom.
I am two fish behind glass, oval and curved. I'm a crack in the parquet filled with crumbs.
I'm tasteless and colorless.
I'm a molecule that belongs to the chair on which I'm sitting, I feed on bad memories. I'm far below with the roots of the irises. The belly

inside the field. Muscle fibers in a slice of earth. Meat of self in mush of soil. Little block of natal-gray. That's how I see it.

It's beautiful.

Everything is in everything. It's marvelous, I feed on bad memories, like the trout feeds feeds feeds on the fly. I'm here and I'm staying.

The woman who always sits at the end of the table, I've been noticing her for quite some time now. A redhead with a big nose and big feet. Her freckles are like bees or like the sun on grass filtered through the leaves or like ants on a pear, or bugs in a salad.

I will have her.

I inch along hugging the wall breathing lest I carry the aspic trembling.

I enter.

Rapid verification. She's there. It's definitely her.

She's more beautiful in reality. Perfect freckles.

I see her in color.

I love her.

Fourteen hours 45 minutes. Coffee. Approach tray. Dodge table. Grasp coffeepot. Pour. Suppress desire to raise pot higher and higher while pouring.

All I have to do is coax the redhead into my room under some excuse or other.

You must be hot? No? You're all right?

Keeping a perfectly straight face, jostle her and fall against her, caressing her breasts, scent = such and such % of and such and such % of. Temperature = X degrees. Consistency = so much +/- elasticity. Sensation of bones below = ?. Fall asleep under the onslaught of emotion.

Wake up naked. Sodomy. Double penetration, finger in the anus + fellatio, licking feet, biting thighs, etc.

We'll do it.

Operation "Freckles."

Closer and closer together toward the bridge of her nose

Eyes blackbird black.

Aaaaaaaaaaare you zeeee gagagardener?
Shovel in one hand, rake in the other, reply ready:
Affirmative and what's more I'm going to show you something. Find the mistake, I'll say to her, as I lead her tip-top speed.
She's flying along horizontally like Peter Pan's sister, streaming through the sky as if an airplane door had suddenly opened. Landing in front of a bench of white roses, in the middle of which I've placed a single red one.
Find the mistake.

Eeet's eeet's eeet's zeee red one.

Very good, Ô yes, very good. It's just like you, Mystery within this Ocean of Banality. And just when she blinks her eyes in surprise,

What the hell are you doing down there?

Looking at me questioning, black eyebrows coming together + dark rings = eyes of dead owl.

Today. Phase II. You want to make progress? You think it's enough to listen at keyholes and overhear a thing or two in the hallways? There's better way to find out what they really think. Reconstruction. It's statistically proven. Suppose I say, adopting the (SVG), Standard Guest Voice: The weather's perfect but tomorrow there will be (...) ? There will be (...) ?
News!
A storm you idiot. Fill in the blanks yourselves. Accumulate information against a minimal margin of error. Moral: We Must Communicate. We live in a society that suffers from a deficit of communication. That's where I got the idea. A newspaper. The (DICN) Daily Internal and Confidential News.
Covering everything that the Quality thinks, supports and wants. (every evening: paper produced afterhours—which means off-the-clock). Working more in order to work better equals?
Working less.

And there we have it—a mere man with a stride of a giant.

CHORUS *(Repeated as accompaniment)*:
I'll sue you / you idiot

No, you're quite wrong there.
It's all wrong,
I tell you, utterly, entirely wrong.
Now, now, ha, ha, temper, temper.
Want to see my temper?
Pass me the sauce.

Do it.
I can influence him at a distance, he knows I'm watching him, mentally I stick pins into his wax effigy.

CHORUS:
Pass me the sauce.

He gets it. It's a code, he's telling me to pass him the knife, he's going to kill him. I pass the vegetables counterclockwise.
Utter silence.
Horrified look from the person at the end of the table. She's starting to feel not so good. I'll save her. She signals to me. She gives me a little wink.
That's the signal.
You just have to pay attention. She's on my side. I knew it. I'm gonna save her. We'll escape together. We'll run away across the fields. We'll outsmart the dogs. We'll walk along through the stream to diffuse our scent.
White skin not used to sun.
You'd better cover yourself. Here, take this, handing her some sort of animal skin. Discretely help her to undress in order to take a census of her freckles.
File it in the memory folder.
Goose pimples.

I-I-I'm c-c-c-cold.

Don't move an inch. I'm going to gather wood for a fire. We'll have to camp here tonight. I know, I know, but that's just the way it is. In case of danger, it's necessary to recreate a hierarchy. Just remember your classics. There has to be a leader. Number one, that's me.

That reminds me of one of my men who had an amazing sense of humor, one day we're up in the air and the guys down below start firing. Bang! They hit our right engine. And so my navigator, one of our boys from the second Zouaves turns to me and you know what he says? Just like that he says: "So long, Colonel." Nowadays things have changed. You start to understand why our veterans are so bitter.

The human being, nonetheless remains capable of noble actions. Certainly, of course. But then two years later you read in the newspaper that this same saint has shot his entire family before "Turning the Gun on Himself."

So give me a break with your fond memories of war. You fucking bastard.

What?

You heard me fucking bastard. Want it spelled out and signed, Colonel?

(Barking.) Finish up that rabbit, there's a carrot hidden in the bullet hole. Whoever finds it first gets the prize.

Night four miles. Twelve mph. I'm doing fine. Thirty-seven strides / minute. Paper fly, bone machine, finish up that rabbit finish up that rabbit. Get those calf ligaments going 422. Accelerate, then breathe.

Run.

Five miles. Blind descent right into the sound of black water. Diver bomber into the black. Batman, that's me. My cape deployed like wings I'm going to get out of this nightmare. I'm a bird cheep-cheep

I'm a scurrying mouse squeak-squeak I'm both. I'm equipped with radar that tells me where everything is in real time. I slide through touching nothing. I'm in time.

Six miles.

I am vegetal, I don't eat what others eat click-clack I fly.

Low-flying grass skimming machine-tool.

Remote control.

I fly therefore I am, etc.

Seven miles.

I think of her, I think of her. I fooled myself. She's a real person.

Ten miles. I stop to breathe. I field dance body cipher warnings. Arms extended in a cross = help / come get me. Standing, legs apart, one arm raised = it's ok / forget me.

When they see it from above, they'll get it.

But I'm too small, they'll never see me. I've shrunk into nature. Wooden soldier against a wall of trees. To become trees to become the trees to become a tree to become the tree. Me lost among transparencies. You can't be everything. Eleven miles. It's not so bad. I'm amazed by the sky no matter what it's doing.

She's a real person.

I didn't realize it. It's not my fault. Fourteen miles. I'm going to save her. Faster. You're a real person.

I am not completely therefore I run. Everything works. Eye muscles too. It's the first time I've seen in color.

The black and white of the past is over.

Here and now it's fabulous.

The eyes' color cells activated. The special blood that constructs 3-D vision. Fifteen miles. I'm the same density as the water. Lead color + night color. But you can't be everything.

And that's all right.

We've got to stop here.

Private, what makes the green grass grow?

Blood, sir, red fresh blood!

That's what being a leader's about, be reassuring, but firm. Don't listen to subalterns and their whining.

With time of course you learn how to minimize the suffering.

What? Do you think a general stays at the front lines just waiting for a bullet? No way, he's back there in his tent. Thinking things over. Stretched out on a leather couch. Or standing in front of a model of the battlefield. Like it should be done.

If he gets killed, who's going to plan the campaign? I've got to make myself a new and much more visible uniform. Got to stand out from the troops. So I can stay in my tent and fully concentrate on the next move. I never sleep. I work too much. My new uniform is red and black, plumed helmet, steel-pointed boots, life is beautiful, I think of everything.

Gentlemen, we've got to get in gear, the numbers have fallen. Satisfaction is down. Heads are going to roll. Some of you have been sacrificing the group for your personal gain, and that, that is going to stop. It's o-ver.

We're going to organize maneuvers. Any one who doesn't go along with it is out of here. Insubordination. Court martial. I'll admit it—I'm pissed. All right, then. Onto the maneuvers. If you can't keep up, we'll throw you a grenade. Blue against white. Bamboo cages for the losers.

Bamboo cages?

Enough with trimming the hedges—we're going to do something big. Real bullets.

Ddrrring!

What the hell are you doing staring at that fucking wall? I've been calling you for an hour, what the hell do you think this thing is for???

Ooooooo dear, true, true—it's the red light, which means Library, blinking away, and so is the one for the Yellow Room.

It was then I realized all wasn't going as planned.

Knock knock.

No reply, maybe he's sleeping? I open the door.
Hmmm, here's your mended vest. I added a bulletproof titanium lining. All set for the next battle. Ha-ha.

What time is it? What on earth are you doing? Why did you turn on the light?

Hair on end + saucer eyes.

What time is it???

You know about electronic microscopes?

What time is it? Are you nuts or what?

Deep into the green and red jungle. Let's go. Onward! I can't. Leave me, comrades. I can't go on. My leg, etc. Kill me, I'll only hold you back.
Go on, kill me.
Off we go. The two battalions march in file dressed in full battle gear. These admirable men execute a superb battle march under a hail of projectiles, shouldering their arms, as if on parade, keeping in line, tadidadidadidadida. Meanwhile, almost immediately, there, a fusillade resounds among the underbrush.
And there ffffffffff watttchhh outtttt ffffff booooom.
The neutron bomb, comrades, a weapon that is transforming the very concept of strategy.
Thirty-six hundred turn. So the neutron bomb combines classic security with modern virtue. Everything living is killed, but material goods are left unharmed. Absolutely untouched. The flowers in their vase, the tea in its teapot, the eggs in their carton.
Citation: these courageous men mowed down by the shards of the iniquitous shell will remain forever as ()? Knight Forever on reserve. Stop.

Knock knock.

I go in.

Gentlemen, do you know this man? Negative. (Response of a group of men in uniform + cigars + cognac.)

Well he's our man.

The admiral. The lieutenant of the 405th. The only man for the job. The crème de la crème. The cream of the cream. He's our man. Applause. Bravo.

Cheers.

See? See? The bullet entered through the stomach. Went through the liver, ricocheted against the shoulder blade and came to lodge itself here.

Feel this bump here?

He's asleep. He doesn't really want to wake up. His breathing's really weird, only inhaling one time out of two. He exhales twice. Inhales once.

I was thinking, that all we'd have to do is attach a tie-mic to M, link it up to a loudspeaker in the office, and work out an easy-to-use code for all circumstances. "Beautiful day today" means "Change the silverware." "Oh, yes …" means "more bread." Advantage: no more foot bell or Morse Code.

Greek Chorus:

Oh yes
Beautiful day today
Blue sky

More bread / Change the silverware / More vegetables!!!

Greek Chorus:

Ah, such lovely flowers
Ha ha ha so amusing
It's the season

Fingerbowl! / Fish! / Error #3 (a spill! a spill!)

Greek Chorus:
A spill! A spill!

The code to the safe. The way is clear. The code? L.O.V.E. = M, pretty obvious if you know him. A bunch of black and white photos of men in officers' uniforms from? This is my mission. I believe in what I do, they'll never know it's me because I don't know it myself.
This is my real job.
Every movement timed and precise. Back erect. Eyes straight forward. Ear volume to maximum. No sweat. No hesitation.

What the hell are you doing there?
It's M in a dressing gown, a .32 pointed my way.
I look at him blankly and then glance down, he glances down too. I give him a triple flying punch right in the face, then just as he's going down, I give him my right under the sternum. He's on his knees with a mouth full of blood, and I finish him off with the poker, which I wash to remove traces of bone and hair.

Greek Chorus:
What did God say
he said go down into the garden
you'll see this and that
all right then this and that I made it all

God said do it in memory of me
so go on do it
but if on the contrary God doesn't add
don't do it in memory of me
by all means don't do it

And if God says nothing at all and adds nothing
do nothing
do nothing at all

All is just fine, except my hands are a little weak. I'm slowing down, I drink too much. You shouldn't drink, you should work out, I'm taking too long. Got to speed it up. Finish the work, close the safe.

It's D-Day I'll tell her: We'll take a room in the first hotel we can find. Gray sheets, flowered bedspreads. Metal furniture. I take the sawed-off Ithaca Mag 10 out of my bag and place a box of cartridges on the left pillow.

What are you doing?

Wait till I come back. Don't open the door. If someone tries to break it down with a hatchet, fire away.

I turn back and slip a couple of slow-combustion grenades under her elbow.

What are these for?

(Screaming.) What the hell do you think? I'm getting you out of this dump! Who the hell do you think's going to get you out of this dump?!

Y-y-y-you.

All right then. Follow instructions. When you fire wear this.

I hand her my steel vest.

You fire, see, bam-bam, and it recoils. Breaks your ribs. There, wear it.

What are you going to do?

That's not quite it, though. Something's not quite right. It's not real life. I feel like it's not my life I'm living. I don't have a life. It's not a life. I have no life. It's not my life.

Anyway, eat this.

I take two tuna fish sandwiches out of my bag. I'll be back.

We'll rent an apartment.

Sitting on a folding metal chair in front of the little window looking out into the courtyard. Sounds of breakfast + rattling dishes + competing radios pouring out the windows, linking the kitchens. Everything is in everything. It's marvelous. I will dispel bad memories. Here + never different + we here + beautiful day = ?

She's asleep.

She's sleeping because she's bored. I'm not fun enough. That's it. That's my problem. Because I have to prepare our future life, D-day = zero.

I'm sorry I did it, you know.

I know.

I don't have a house. Have you thought about that? Have you *really* thought about it?

Yes.

Oh thank you, thank you so much. And again, bravo for the stuttering. It adds such an air of authenticity. I love you enormously.

Me too.

Me too. You're my super-sister.

Thanks.

Oh kiss me there

Oh kiss kiss me there.

We'll have a peaceful life. What do you want for dinner? Rabbit? Coming right up. Bang-bang. Rabbit on fire, paws neatly tucked up. House salad. Apple wine. Hand-dried tobacco. Hammock. I'll love you forever, *even in a city*. I have an honest face. My words match my tone. I talk neither too loudly nor too much. No weird twitches or squints.

For a moment, nothing happens. Don't pressure her. Don't exaggerate. No point in overdoing it.

And if it was he?
If the unknown guest was the Colonel?
But it was he. Ever since the beginning. And, I didn't see a thing. I passed him in the hallway, and he looked straight at me then winked *just after*. He winked at me.
That's the signal. Got to admit, I didn't catch on for a minute. What a pro. I keep telling myself he must have been doing it from the start. Remarkable. A real artist. What a brilliant idea—to act like a total idiot.

Knock-knock.

Come in.

I've got them Colonel.

What?

(Whispering.) Listen, I've got to tell you, even if it's not my place (number one obey without thinking of the consequences, number two reserve duty, number three disappear upon failure at ground zero.) I've got to warn you that those photos are of no interest whatsoever. Just personal stuff, family, vacations, etc. No submarine plans. Just a bunch of people swimming, that's all.
This isn't the Eagle's nest.
Speaking of that, brilliant cover. Ingenious, that playing the utter idiot bit. Remarkable.
"Such beautiful September light. But watch out nippy in the evenings. This rumor about winter is ridiculous. Better cover the dogs."
Listen, there must be some mistake. I don't get the point, what's this mission all about? But what had to be done is done. No discussion. No one's seen anything. Even if I did go a little too far. But it's only normal to want to improve things. To want to adapt to local customs.

(Loud.) When in Rome, do like the Romans.
After so much listening at keyholes, you become a spy. Or else it's the other way around. It's the egg that makes the chicken. It's too much.

I laugh. *(He laughs.)*

Unless there was a code. You put the first names of each one end to end going clockwise and—!—you've got the word H.E.L.P. That's it.
I get it.
He's acting like he knows nothing. He's a real pro. He's trying to tell me that the place is bugged. And me, telling all.
(Loud.) Perhaps it's a good time to change them?
The flowers. There's a microphone in the flowers.
Not a bad idea. Certainly sir. You've seen the team. I've trained them from the bottom up for D-day. Mentally superior. Third generation. They don't even know what they're doing but they'll do it all right. No questions asked. No more mission. Just pure work.
Or else he's trying to tell me I'm fired. That's it. It's over. It could happen to anybody. Just because you're from the other side, they automatically think you're going to work for them anyway. They fire you with no warning, and you continue. You stay there forever not knowing that it's over. Useless night patrols. Throw away the plans. Too much gear. Voluntary exile. Forced celibacy. Great body for nothing.

Bring me a plate of cold meat and pickles, please.

The cold war I understand, sir.

That's right. With pickles.

Opening his paper.

You like her, don't you? The little redhead.

I understand. Good. A new mission. Things don't stop just like that. They're satisfied with my work after all.
If I start something, I see it through to the end. I never forget my duty. I did well not to escape with her.
She's not on our side.
It's perfectly clear. I understand it all. I almost fell into the trap.
Incredible.

What if I go in disguise? Brilliant. Now that I know the whole story.
I phone from inside the house feigning an exterior call.
(Inaudibly, sort of Roubonsoon. Handkerchief over the mouthpiece.) Hello my dear sir. Colonel +++++ here.

Chorus: What?

(Hyper-distinctly pinching his nose.) Rahhh-biiinn-sonnnn.

Chorus: Excuse me but I can hardly hear you.

I'm a friend of your friend *(Rapidly.)* Kannverstehen.

Chorus: Sorry, I didn't quite catch the name.

(Snapping nasally, even faster.) Kannverstehen.

Chorus: Ah, yes, of course, yes certainly. Delighted.

It just so happens that I'm in your area for a few days on maneuvers. A real circus. We've got the guys from the second Zouaves and the whole nine yards, helicopter, etc.

Chorus: Fabulous. Uh, can you come by for lunch?

That'll be something.

Chorus: What? I can't hear you very well.

I said, with pleasure. I was just congratulating myself on the coincidence that made me choose to—how can I put it—carry out my patriotic duty in your neck of the woods. That reminds me of something a certain dictator said about us; he said something like, "They're a country of small farmers who could lead the fashion industry," and you know he's not entirely wrong, though a few things have changed.

But not all that much, eh? That'd be something if things had really changed eh? Things never change eh? Re-arm 'em and send 'em back out.

Laugh.

CHORUS: Uh, yeah, right, I gotta say (...) It's true that, today, well (...)

No need to explain. Welcome a little calm eh? Feeling a bit overextended? Just when you need an eagle's eye and a wolf's stride.

CHORUS: Whaaaat?

The situation's bad really bad and you need nerves of steel, eh? From what I hear you're really really well organized. What time?

Laugh again.

CHORUS: One o'clock.

And I take it your daughter'll be there?

CHORUS: My daughter?

Yeah, the little redheaded number. What time?

CHORUS: One o'clock.

Delighted, etc.

CHORUS:

Wake up	Wake up early.
Rent	Rent a fast car.
Turn	Turn into the drive between the open gates.
Floor it	Floor it 7400 rpm's. Several miles into the dark tunnel of over-hanging trees.
Break. Emerge in full light.	Break out of the trees. Emerge in full light.
Double clutch.	Double clutch. Slight skid around in a 146 degree arc. No tracks left in the plush gravel.
Cut	Cut the engine.
Leap	Leap over the low door, legs first followed by the
Zip. Twist	head levered by the arms. Zip. Twist of the hips,
Land.	and land both feet on the ground.

11 *September* 2001

Michel Vinaver

AUTHOR'S NOTE

Text written in the weeks following the destruction of the Twin Towers in Manhattan. Written in English (more precisely, in American), no doubt because of the location of the event and because English is the language of the words taken from daily newspapers. French version then written by the author.

The form is close to that of the cantata and oratorio, composed of arias (for one, two, or three voices), choral parts (which, in the French version, remain in the original language), and recitatives spoken by a "journalist," whose function may recall that of the evangelist in the Passions by J. S. Bach.

"Who is speaking?" The names of the characters must be heard or seen: they have the same status as the words.

CHARACTERS

Unidentified Male Voice from the Cockpit of American Airlines Flight 11
Air Traffic Controller
Pilot of United Airlines Flight 175
Unidentified Pilot
Voice from Crew of the Military C-130 Cargo Plane
Chorus
Madeline Sweeney
Michael Woodward
Todd Beaver

Lisa
Bush
Journalist
Katherine Ilachinski
Judy Wein
Nat Alamo
Richard Jacobs
Rumsfeld
Instruction Sheet to Hijackers
Dorene Smith
John Paul DeVito
Arturo Domingo
Atta
First Trader
Second Trader
Jan Demczur
Iyer
Bin Laden
Young Female Voice

PLACE
Manhattan in the weeks following the destruction of the Twin Towers. September 11, 2001.

Unidentified Male Voice from the Cockpit of American Airlines Flight 11
(Slight Arab accent.)
We have some planes
Just stay quiet
And you'll be OK
We are returning to the airport

Air Traffic Controller
Who's trying to call me?

Silence.

THE UNIDENTIFIED MALE VOICE
Nobody move please
We are going back to the airport
Don't try to make any stupid moves

PILOT UNITED AIRLINES FLIGHT 175
We heard
A suspicious transmission on our departure from Boston
Sounds like
Someone keyed the mike and said
Everyone stay in your seats

AIR TRAFFIC CONTROLLER
There's no transponder
No nothing
And no one's talking to him

UNIDENTIFIED PILOT
Anybody know
What that smoke is in lower Manhattan?

Silence.

AIR TRAFFIC CONTROLLER
We may
Have a hijack
We have
Some problems over here right now

Silence.

American 77 Indy
American 77 Indy radio check
How do you read?

Silence.

A fast-moving primary target
Is moving east
Heading toward the forbidden airspace over the White House the Capitol and the Washington
Monument

Silence.

Intercept and identify the fast moving target

VOICE FROM CREW OF THE MILITARY C-130 CARGO PLANE
It's a Boeing 757
Moving low and fast

CHORUS
One More Night
The Ultimate Check-out
Enjoy a Complimentary Fourth Night
At One of
The Leading Hotels of the World
Rising and Falling
A Boom and a Bust
The Slump but a Rebound

FEMALE VOICE
Madeline Sweeney speaking
I'm a flight attendant aboard American Airline 11

MALE VOICE
Michael Woodward here
Ground manager Logan Airport hi Madeline

MADELINE
Michael this plane
Has been hijacked
They have just gained access to the cockpit
The plane's now reversed direction
It's begun now reversed direction
It's begun to descend rapidly

ANOTHER MALE VOICE
Operator?

OPERATOR
Hi

THE OTHER MALE VOICE
Hello what's your name?

OPERATOR
Lisa

THE OTHER MALE VOICE
For God's sake this is incredible you've got the same name as my wife
Listen Lisa my name's Beaver
Todd Beaver

LISA
Hi Todd

MICHAEL
Do you know your location Madeline?

MADELINE
I see water and buildings
Oh my God oh my God

Sound: The crash of an airplane.

TODD
Listen carefully Lisa I know I'm going to die

LISA
What do you mean?

TODD
I'm on United Airline 93 headed to San Francisco we've been hijacked

LISA
You're crew or passenger?

TODD
Passenger we've heard
About the two hijacked airliners that slammed into the World Trade Center a quarter of an hour ago

LISA
Oh you have

TODD
Yeah
We're heading toward the same sort of destination
The White House possibly
We're going to resist it
They've herded all of us into a galley at the rear

CHORUS
After the Walkout
The Next Mideast Descent
Battle Heats Up
A New Kind of Mission as the U.S. Stands Back
One More Night
The President's Advisers Have Been Working
To Present Him as a More Commanding Leader
Slowdown Forcing Bush to Shift Focus

Todd

Yes this includes the two pilots who are injured
They've stabbed one passenger to death
There are three of them or maybe four one of them is standing guard over us
With a bomb attached to his waist
We're going to do something
Jump on him then hopefully run to the cockpit
One of us is a trained pilot a V.P. of Connecticut-based Safe Flight Instrument Company
Please Lisa relay a message to Lisa my wife tell her I love her and the boys

Chorus

Memo from Wall Street Even Harder Path Ahead
Oracle Chief Sees Few Survivors in PC Shakeout
Abrasive Day in Court Kabul in an Extraordinary Collision of Cultures

Todd

And that I love the boys David is three and Drew is one
She's expecting a third it will be a girl in January
Pray for me

Chorus

Fragile Beauty Under Assault

Todd

Are you guys ready?
Let's roll

Sound: The crash of an airplane.

Chorus

Hi
Jacked

Hi
Jacked Jets Jackety Jets
Hijacked Jets
Hi
Jets Hit Trade
World Weird
Worlderly Trade
Pentagon
Twin Towers
Falling Down Falling Down Falling
Gone
The Twin Towers Are Falling Down Falling Down
Falling Down

BUSH
Freedom itself
Was attacked this morning by a faceless coward
And freedom
Will be defended

CHORUS
Amid horror and disbelief

BUSH
I want to reassure the American people

CHORUS
How Have You Been?
We're Out
Get Away from it All
Well
For an Hour or Two

BUSH
Make no mistake

CHORUS
The People You Need are Only a Touch Away
Attackers Neither Mad nor Desperate

BUSH
The United States will hunt down
And punish
Those responsible for these cowardly acts

CHORUS
U.S. Terror Alert Networks
Were Looking in the Wrong Direction
Warnings
Went Unheeded for Years

BUSH
We have taken the necessary precautions
To continue the functions of your government

CHORUS
Buildings
Were Unprepared to Withstand such an Impact

BUSH
The resolve
Of our great nation is being tested
But make no mistake

CHORUS
Paths
Of Terror a Nation
Mourns

BUSH
We will show the world
God bless

JOURNALIST
Here I am standing
At Ground Zero I behold
Scenes of chaos and fear
Some are alive some are dead some were alive

CHORUS
Bush Vows to Hunt Down Perpetrators

JOURNALIST
People were seen
Falling from upper floors of the 110-story buildings

CHORUS
Amid the Chaos Extraordinary Choices

JOURNALIST
Voluntarily
Or was it the blast
Shall we ever know?

FEMALE VOICE
My name's Katherine Ilachinski I'm 70 I'm an architect
My office is
I should say was
On the 91st floor of Two World Trade Center
The south tower that is
That was
I was knocked off my chair by the blast of heat exploding from the neighboring tower
What should I do? It's them not us nevertheless I figured get out fast
So I went for the stairs

OTHER FEMALE VOICE
My name's Judy Wein
Same tower 103rd floor

I suppose I screamed I set off too

MALE VOICE
My name's Nat Alamo
Working with Morgan Stanley
I'd been on the phone with my fiancée
She told me to flee
As I made my way down
I ignored the official with the megaphone of the 44th floor who said
Go back up you're safe here
Moments later my tower was struck
I went down three steps at a time
Flying

OTHER MALE VOICE
My name's Richard Jacobs I'm with Fuji Bank
I left the 79th floor with all my colleagues
On the 48th floor we heard the announcement that the situation was under control
Several got in the elevators and went back up
Two minutes or so before the second plane smashed into their floor
I just don't know what happened to them

RUMSFELD
Ultimately they're going to collapse from within
That is what will constitute victory

JOURNALIST
Amid the uncertainty about the best thing to do
Some left others stayed
Some began the climb down and when met with the announcement
Went back up
The decisions made in those instants proved momentous
Because many who opted to stay
Were doomed when the second jet crashed into the south tower

Roughly one hour elapsed
Between the first strike and the fall of the last of the two towers

INSTRUCTION SHEET TO HIJACKERS
The last night
Remind yourself that in this night
You will face many challenges
But you have to face them
And understand it one hundred percent
Obey God
His messenger

JOURNALIST
Decisions made during those 60 minutes
Helped determine if people perished or lived

INSTRUCTION SHEET
And don't fight among yourselves
Where you become weak
And stand fast

JOURNALIST
Without question the evacuation of thousands of people
Went well
People helping each other with acts of courage great and modest

INSTRUCTION SHEET
God will stand
With those who stood fast
Purify your heart and clean it from all earthly matters
The time of fun and waste has gone

JOURNALIST
People on floors as high as the 88th in the north tower
Stepping on bodies and rubble
Made the full trip to safety

INSTRUCTION SHEET
You have to be convinced that those few hours
That are left you in your life
Are very few

JOURNALIST
In the packed stairwell
People stepped aside to let burn victims speed past

INSTRUCTION SHEET
From there you will begin to live
The happy life
The infinite paradise

JOURNALIST
People who made it out depict a scene of carnage
Calm and some confusion
About what to do

INSTRUCTION SHEET
Be optimistic
The prophet was always optimistic
Check all your items
Your bag your clothes
Knives
Your will
Your IDs your passport your safety
Make sure nobody is following you
When you enter the plane
O God open all doors for me
O God you who open all doors

FEMALE VOICE
My name is Dorene Smith
I was standing at my desk on the 88th floor there with a colleague

Instruction Sheet
Please open all doors for me
Open all avenues to me

Dorene
When parts of the ceiling caved in
We're going to be fine we told each other as we grabbed our pocketbooks
And moved through the rubble to the stairway

Male Voice
My name is John Paul DeVito

Dorene
At the 78th floor I saw a woman whose hair and clothing
Had largely been burned off

John Paul
I was sitting down to some paperwork and a second cup of coffee after meeting with a client

Dorene
She was aflame I couldn't hold her so I held a sweater around her waist

Other Male Voice
My name's Arturo Domingo

John Paul
And next to me was Harry Ramos it was 8:48 a.m. when our building

Dorene
And guided her down amid debris and this special smell of singed wood

Arturo
I work with Morgan Stanley

John Paul
Lurched violently like a ship in high seas
Mr. Ramos our head trader

Dorene
Several hundred others stepped out of the way to let us pass

Arturo
The descent had been calm and orderly

John Paul
Braced himself in the doorway I was nearly knocked off my chair I run this outfit as chief operating officer not a big outfit we've had a few problems

Dorene
And we made it to the street in 18 minutes

Arturo
But when I reached the 44th floor a man with a megaphone
Stood there telling people there was no problem his exact words were
"Our building is secure you can
Go back to your floor
If you're a little winded
You can
Get a drink of water or coffee in the cafeteria"

John Paul
Lighting fixtures pulled loose from the ceiling crashing on the floor papers flew smoke poured in through holes that suddenly opened overhead several employees screamed
Neither Harry nor me had any idea what had happened Harry was just back from a week's leave after the death of his mother-in-law a bomb we thought the main problem was that smoke
I called Marilyn my wife

"I love you Mar" I said "I love our kids take care of the kids"
Harry Ramos and me we're two normal men each with 25 years on Wall Street
Trying to slug out a living in a bear market
I'm 45 years old the son of immigrants with two school-age daughters and a house in Chappaqua New York
And Mr. Ramos approaching his 45th birthday on Sunday lived in Newark
I say lived because he is dead
I suppose anyway
He had been staying behind
Directing confused strangers into the stairwell
Finally outside
Engulfed by smoke and dust I don't know if I'm going to survive this I thought
I began walking with my eyes closed bumping into parked cars falling down picking myself up
Weeping alive ecstatic about life glad I had decided to help others to safety grieving about Ramos

JOURNALIST
People in the south tower
Had less time to make a choice
Last to be hit first to collapse

CHORUS
Sifting Through the Aftermath
Wall Street Weighs Timing of Job Cuts
DNA Testing Doctors Hope
Will Help to Identify the Dead

ATTA
This is my will
Those who will sit beside my body
Must pray for me
To be with the angels

JOURNALIST
The 19 men prepared for their final day
In a tight choreography
Over 18 months

ATTA
The body is to be washed and wrapped
In three pieces of white cloth
Not to be made from silk or expensive material

A TRADER
I think quite candidly

ATTA
The person who will wash my body near the genitals

THE TRADER
That it's better to have more time between the disaster and the reopening of the financial markets

JOURNALIST
Only one aboard each of the four commandeered aircraft
Knew how to fly a plane

THE TRADER
The more time that we get to think about this and to think logically
The more rational response will be in the markets

ATTA
Must wear gloves on his hands
So he won't touch my genitals

ANOTHER TRADER
I expect it to be a time of heavy volatility

First Trader
As I see it damage to the stock market will be limited
The United States is a very big country
With a huge and diverse economy

Chorus
The Physics of Turning a Tower into a Cloud of Dust and Rubble

Atta
I don't want a pregnant woman or a person who is not clean
To come and say good-bye to me
I don't want any woman to come to my grave at all during my funeral or on any occasion thereafter

Journalist
Mohamed Atta when he wrote his will five years earlier
Did not know
That there would be no body

Chorus
On Wall Street
Times are Difficult
Jobs Have to be Cut
Yet Most Companies are Reluctant
To Dismiss People Immediately
For Fear of Seeming Heartless

Bush
It is vital
To keep consuming

Chorus
Keep Desires Afloat

Bush
Keep buying

To preserve the economy
From collapsing

CHORUS

For This is War Prepare
To Suffer Hardships
Consent Sacrifices

JOURNALIST

Now memories orbit around small things
None of the other window washers liked his old and rusty green bucket
But Jan Demczur
Found its rectangular mouth
Perfect for dipping and wetting his squeegee
In one motion
The time was 8:47 A.M.
With five other men
Shivan Iyen John Paczkowski George Pheonix Colin Richardson
And another man whose identity could not be learned
Mr. Demczur boarded car 69A
An express elevator that stopped on floors 67 through 74
The car rose
But before it reached the level of its first potential landing

DEMCZUR

We felt a muted thud
The building shook
The elevator swung from side to side
Like a pendulum

IYER

Then it plunged
In the car someone punched an emergency stop button
The elevator cabin stopped
Smoke seeped in

Journalist
They succeeded in prying apart the car doors

Iyer
But there was no exit
Facing us a blank wall stenciled with the number "50"

Journalist
Demczur sliding his squeegee's metal edge against the wall back and forth over and over
Was able to cut a rectangle about 30 by 45 centimeters

Iyer
It was 9:30 by this time the 50th floor was already deserted Demczur wouldn't drop his bucket as we stumbled down the rubble "the company might not order me another one" he said

Journalist
As the descent was getting rougher requiring the use of hands roundabout the 21st floor he had to let it go
At 10:23 they burst onto the street five minutes later the north tower collapsed
Their escape had taken 95 of the one hundred minutes between the plane's crash and the building's collapse

Iyer
If the elevator had stopped at the 60th instead of the 50th floor we would've been five minutes too late
That man with the squeegee he was like our guardian angel

Bush
Good afternoon on my orders the United States military has begun strikes

Bin Laden
Here is America struck by God Almighty in one of its vital organs

BUSH
We are supported in this operation by the collective will of the world

BIN LADEN
So that its greatest buildings are destroyed grace and gratitude to God

BUSH
Now the Taliban will pay a price initially the terrorists may burrow deeper into caves

BIN LADEN
America has been filled with horror from north to south and east to west

BUSH
Our military action is designed to clear the way for sustained comprehensive and relentless

BIN LADEN
And thanks be to God that what America is tasting

BUSH
Operations to drive them out and bring them to justice

BIN LADEN
Is only a copy of what we have tasted

BUSH
At the same time the oppressed people of Afghanistan will know the generosity of America

BIN LADEN
God has blessed a group of vanguard Muslims to destroy America

BUSH
As we strike military targets we will also drop food

BIN LADEN
May God allot them a supreme place in heaven

BUSH
The United States of America is a friend of the Afghan people

BIN LADEN
Then the whole world went into an uproar the infidels followed by the hypocrites

BUSH
And we are the friends of almost a billion worldwide who practice the Islamic faith

BIN LADEN
Hypocrisy raised its head up high bemoaning those killers who toyed with the blood honor and sanctities of Muslims

BUSH
We're a peaceful nation

BIN LADEN
They backed the butcher against the victim the oppressor against the innocent child

BUSH
In the face of today's new threat the only way to pursue peace

BIN LADEN
The wind of change is blowing

BUSH
Is to address those who threaten it

BIN LADEN
To remove evil

Bush
The name of today's military operation

Bin Laden
I swear to God

Bush
Is Enduring Freedom

Bin Laden
That America will not live in peace

Bush
Our patience in all the sacrifices that may come

Bin Laden
Before all the army of infidels depart the land of Muhammad

Bush
The battle is now joined

Bin Laden
God is the greatest

Bush
We will not waver

Bin Laden
These events have divided the world

Bush
We will not tire

Bin Laden
Into two camps

Bush
We will not falter

Bin Laden
The camp of the faithful

Bush
And we will not fall

Bin Laden
And the camp of the infidels

Bush
Peace and freedom will prevail

Bin Laden
May God shield us

Bush
May God continue to bless us

Young Female Voice
Sure yes sure I ought to've been at the office
Thank God Tommy had an indigestion he vomited all night
Got me really worried why don't you take the day off Paul said for once get a little rest
I can't do that to him Paul I said there's this closure meeting at ten Mr. Gainsborough expects me to get his files ready for the ultimate details
Sometimes the trickiest in a negotiation of this nature
Seven billion dollars in stock and three-and-a-half in cash plus four point eight in debt a pretty flamboyant operation
There'll always be this meeting or that meeting honey Paul said to me Mr. Gainsborough will understand take a look at yourself in the mirror you're not fit I swear
All right I said
And now and now and now

Adramelech's Monologue

Valère Novarina

Translated by Guy Bennett

CHARACTERS

Adramelech

In dire straits, Adramelech grips the bliss engine's drive wheel by the prop and gives it a spin. His monologue is massive. Get to it!

Adramelech: Sufferin' sycophant! Sufferin' sulfurous supine simian syllogist! The Adramelech's toil's hit its peak. Adramelech! … Sire? I made you of clay. And I go where? To shelter 'neath your splint'ry coat and gnaw your soon-sluiced stump. Hail yes, I'm there lickety-split. So I says to the guy who'd ogle me through spy-like specs. Nine-fourths of our lives wasted in inane hours of stanzas, staces, comings, and goings! We lift our arms your head falls off. Ah the disappointment of my life's voyage with its lame stations! My head's too triangular, not round enough for my taste: my arms are good, not long enough though and eight short of ten. Adrameon, Ablamelion, Ablamelech, shut up or step up, but no more words! Marl to my pickaxe, gloss to my heals! We's one thousand below, a handful holds down the fort. They's there in their abode. Their eyes can't see us but we can see them we can, but their eyes can't see us and they can't see us there they can't. Quiet Albert Bellows, crawl quiet, lift your head and give ass! Adrameluce. Watch your mug, you old retorter, it'll spring from my head held high, the talker, gush from my hip, slip from the grave and nip at your ears! The number of our children's dead by scatterment, our big provisions obliterated, ourselves soon gone to disguilegangladon. Cut, go on, shake, speak, through mouth shoot us out with a well-lapped word, a good whistle to unhinge us; with your rattle will you tongue and pierce the air? Answer or whistle, sufferin' song, vibrate! What shall I say? … Don't wanna come when they call. Quiet! Your voice stops progress. Quiet! Your progress stops the vocassonic flight of my voxes! Quiet, Abliblalech, your babbling keeps me from counting your steps! The world's sinking fast! Spare our ears your stupid spurts! Zat guy mumbling or stumbling? Nothing. Grumble, troubled maw. I'm not grumbling, I'm launching a vast clamor from the ship's hold. Hmmm, hmmm, you think he'll really bite? It's wiring, it's wiring! Don't wanna bite, just wanna say. Sufferin' sulfurous simpering sinister supine simian syllogist! Don't wanna bite, just wanna say. Nothing's evolved our positions for too long, no journey no change no morphing from herein, and no thing cackling or copious to disinitiate the extreme leanness of my paltry position. Down with the eternal to and fro of rhythmatic logic. Stop him, boss, he resists and denies galloping. Adramelech! Mmmmm? I made you of clay, ain't that OK? He's bored alone, sire. Shoulda given him a saxus, the jerk. Let's plant some soul by this bolster. Adramelech, you insomniac, here's your saxus. Thanks. And a sister. Thanks. I give you a sister to simmer you down. Good day Miss Manlette, the punctured. Cousin, here's my target. I recognize you, reptat's prey, you've been snatched from the reptant's jaws, sprung from September's bridge. I know it well, cleft open from there myself. No reply? To think, to think the dark star dogs that dark mouth: the nibbler eaten feeds on it and gets big: through this dark mouth I'll speak to the hole myself. Speak and eat it, speak and avenge me through this hole. Brutish bitch of my knees, what's your tongue telling me? Have our homes's walls been swallowed? Do our tunes hit your ears whole? I can't hear you for my ears are wood. Your ugly eyes are gouged out, you she-zebra'd mole. No zebra, for all animals have long left these regions. Then how do you know it's one? The partition's vile trunk. Though who cares about the one who says he snoozes matters isn't late low rather intends to harm, to harm, to harm, to harm, to harm. Death to the white-light'd yellow star that ate the animals! Albumbliton's maldalbulb! Be brave, Mameluke, open the scape and hail the exalted swallower: he'll bear you in his teeth one day. 'Tis like the gourd and its gourdon: error and illusion. The grooved yellow star's suffocating puffing shed naught on my carnage. That brigand had nothing to do with it. For all made I emerged alone. And due to nothing, 'cept badly if not to furious butt-thumping. Of which two globes the dreadful din deafened my childhoods, such that I am still, though hairy and with bearded beak, to this day dazed and confused. The yammering false planet's hammering had nothing to do with it, for I appeared, saber in hand, naked, direct, and uncaftaned. In a word, the old Mameluke ain't about to start kowtowing to the any old one of these days springing up. Sun or no sun, I won't greet him. Look, there's Willoughby in his Model T. Remembers me we shoulda got us some 'fore they closed. Hells bells, where is that flier? And who's a-knocking? Dawn's knocking, you dolt, the first rays of the big squinter. You hear? Dumb old dawn, the first hitcups of that filthy feeler. Repeat after me! 'Tis but the former day come back with its old hee-haw. Hail, hail, harsh star, your lines of bright light pierce the what! Better greet him and thank for the hereabouts so prettily he rilluminates mechanically. Go on, set and rise not again, ugly sun don't come back! A wish he grants toot sweet the punk. Not a ray to be seen, night's already covering me with its seedy ceiling; and here's evening with its falling sun, then day again pointing its ugly whiteness at me, then evening again and it's dark all over. Come back, my pretty blond beauty! Go set you nasty ray! Our shanks sting and want no one see no more nothing. Nor our mugs or yours. And if, ever obedient, it leaves and we we we we return, dragging low our placards low round the neck, whereon, inscribed in alphabetical letters, we read: here lies, breadless, with neither foot nor future, the black figure of poor Stumpton, left here alone, abandoned, while beautiful running suns shine on elsewhere. Mayoose soloose soom. Hey Harriet, where are A.J., Burton, Crucious, and our Louises; where have these other pigeons gone? And et cetera's so forth; so too it goes with summer and winter. And other stuff I slipped Lisa beneath the pillow. And other quips she slipped back, and other words I returned 'til she left me one fine

April day, struck dead by appendicitis. Brazen, beautiful sparrow, soup consoles, peep your big platelette, empty it quick, empty it! Bootless looney feasts. When I stoop to wet my whistle I spy myself suffering. What? I see myself as I see them. Miriam mating with Lucious: dull thud of cold, thump of two butts, thud of crold bods, thump of two globes bootlessly spanked by the frantic man fast out of breath with no air left. Do say, do say! Trop tard! Nothing makes my old mug happier. Do tale, do tale! So glum a child was I that they decked out my slight frame with a puffy face ten times greater. Do stop, do stop! At twice the age or more I was so sad they dubbed me "peelings," an onioniforous allusion to the legumes that, strapping up, I were tearfully peeling in my heart. Do trell, do trell! Batches of stuff in advance whose … Quiet, somebody's there! Who are you? Who's the newbie? Peter Pronto, son of Andy Pronto and Lynne his wife. Here's an encodette with a lettron for you, painted probably with brush, I've seen by transparency. Thanks postmon. Wanna knock back something hot? Want some grub? Why the Pronto name you bear? Whereas everyone knows you as Nordicus? Dog gamn, what does this prattler want with us? The Nordicus moniker's a joke: I'm from the South. And thanks for the broth; just back from a walk, I've boccaccio'd too much already. Relic, what's the inscriptate say? Can't, it's written in knife holes or somesuch. Drops of banal water 'bliterated its characters. Assemblage of squinty signs with transfixed signals. One heck of a wind's blowing outside, but I'm where it's warm. Another glass? Sufferin' myopia! Yayess. 'Tis it not a letter from old Ganglabedus? Yayess … The bouquet on your table reminds me of another, grazed on Alpine pastures by Leon's cow. 'Cept that thereupon, the plants are blacker than those you planted to decorate your domicile. From that there pasture I came into the world and began grandly pumping its air. Thirty foster fathers employed to ensure my trust fought night and day to see who'd cut wood for my fire. Said wood was to keep the animals away. For them this honor being immense, they persevered for years. Right up 'til had, scattered by batrachians and invaded by corvidae, to leave the Alpine meadow and our own. I'd just turned five. We lived in Portsmouth, whose bubbly oshun splashed joyfully at our front walls. With big ears equipped, new, and mighty proud of my young mug, I ran o'er the plain, swinging my flail to eat all the bread! Each evening my brothers left in a massive group, heave-ho-ing their hoop nets from the maritime desert. Each morning their 20 convoys piled high with game and covered with catch returned to us without incident from the Renowned Islands. Our elders greeting us from the sails, we young replied by signs, perched at the pinnacle of the highest pontoons. We had fine weather in those days. Drop it, bottom hole, you're sawing the system! But one day noon struck sudden wild winter and I fled in dense forests to hide my visible body from the sight of all birds. Those black bitches scoured the seas, eyeing our agitates from above. Hidden 'neath a box tree I didn't get et. Spinning overhead and dipping their wings they whooped: "We want Pronto, where's his head, let him come out!" The beasts left that springtime and I saw them fly backwards. They crossed the horizon one evening at seven, peeved at their unlucky hunt. My father blasted then buried them with what German troops remained. Their burial was celebrated by one hundred rounds, under the splashing gay sun. Much wine was wasted. Scoundrelly factotum, you're dogging our ears with this unwinding of stupidass events! If they seem stupid to you, it's because I was only six and at the time everything seemed stupid to me. Reason I got later. On Saint Wearing Saint Breeches Now Day. Facing the virgin God carved in bread, candle held high, erect on two legs and hardly tottering, and at mid-arm, hanging, trickling down, the short white-lace armband, I saw my life pass before my eyes in an asinine dream. Way past swaddling, I drop my rompers, achieve a three-piece, and feel a shroud coming on. Sickened by this perspective, before the present God of the tabernacle, I swore, spewing it all out in front of the boxton, I'd become a human canon, right then on the spot not a second wasted, a filthy assassinating assassin, blasting one crime after another, exterminating near passersby 'til they perch me out on Guillot's tine. Whence I howl as they hack me: "Pipe down, I'm talking to you! He who speaks can be seen on the block. He who speaks from here's striding to his final ah and soon to gasp his last. He'll flow red his head will roll its story unspoken. Birds with navigating feet, and you other navigators of the sea's skin, listen one and all to the last song launched in air. He'll sink head first and in blood taste the bitter taste of the filthy tasting horrors' bitter taste. But, unlike you, who zip out a quick one in your underpants, I depart in public. Setting out for reptat he recalls his coming and brief life in the tiny world. A voyage so short in space so stupid ain't even worth describing. Tightrope walker stooped on scaffold's top, he'll fling this ah from the tip o' the block, to you, turbulent holes below, him above, flings it to you, below, myself swirling, head in ring. It's the dark, virtually round ring that gives nowhere and way down, yes! Those still lively should listen to this ah when I fling it, let it come, stick it to me, the giantess, right in the middle of my meeten's muzzle!" I was about to smash it all, wind up deep in dungeon or 'neath a high black knife, so dark was the black project I lay hatching before the host. 'Twas purely by chance that I eluded embracing a criminal vocation: thanks to the next war's break out, five years I silently served our republics under your flags. From silent battles I returned with one arm less. So since then, so no question of assassinating anybody. Nor in the world to cut my way with flicks o' the knife. Hired by the Postal Office. Hence the Pronto name and Nordicus which I lost. Under hole of not at all, denizens of the deep, old fish, ex-birds and you bottom-dwelling extinguished souls, swallow him in your turbulent waters, may this bottomless being wallow there, may he sink pronto! Disappear child, pass through the nail-door, join Melcher and Moocher! Go, exit, leave the century! The memory of this ferryman fades, good. Night falls, gotta mate up again. Honor and labor of misdeeds and to the misdeeds of the septat and sextat. Let's jig. Night falls and fades the memory of this jerk. A shot o' reptant? Ho field mouse, a shot o' reptus? The ancient old ever-ready feminine artery always wishing another sip. Pour us a full brimming instead, with an eye to nights of long flight, water that mouths that swells our black inners with their howelling animals, those critters are thirsty. Et anticipiat fenestram omnis multitudinem caput. Peep how they burn, yes! They burn a lot of light in town, God knows, a thousand kilowatts, a thousand faradays! a thousand sick people to attend to, to lead lit up 'til dawn for their squeak. Et grabatus omniam semper bragatus. In night's middle they light joyous holes to appease their furibat. Hoists of hook-sacks all furious at the repeated assault of the what. That's the tune. Such is the relentless fuss of the heart. Hup! Hup! Hup! Hup! Hup! Hup! Then no more bouncing. Quarter of a second! For ceaselessly do they tend to recommit the awful act of rogation. That's the tune! Each blow they hurl fills them with visiting child, from whom shoots quick the rectangled violasson that croaks strangled by first click. The child they strangulate is snatched victorious from the grave. Buggerment o' the cask hole! Snatched victorious from the grave. Just born this pale ray neither sees nor hears, yet to it do they say: "Noble child, destroy us and shave off our faces." And said child—how admirable—encapsulates in one round fart both captives' twin features. This child, a blue, one-eyed gimp, straddles the one-eyed, gimpish world. And thus stretch they their splendid things ever higher! In night's middle they light joyous holes. From which we receive, here, spurted from the what, these thousand lines of brief light. Which illuminate this city in millions o' faradays. Pullulate. Tumult. Massive, massive! By Saint Ceiling, dass real martyrdom, Saint Boton style! By Saint Gudule, I see this couple from the depths brutally banging the holy partitions of the minuscule in a concerted and stubborn effort to open the force of the orifice; the latter, unknowing that once it's unbuttoned, its seeker's being hoisted, not it's slit as do they say. Then they keel over and roll on padding, dreadfully eating their partner's tears. Help, through the mouth, now she tricks, dips, pulls it out, he offers back, she removes his, extirpates his, gives out a sound, that he throws her, hatchet-like, aplenty. And with a laugh they swill down each other's bridge, and fall back headless from above. Without a word, get back to it, determined, hopeless, in excessive use of belling Algibuse. He, red, she, dancing, devouring his white him, like ear eats sound. To the very last pirouetto. Furious walse of the bohemio. I see but two bodies prone stone dead stuck on eight pointy pegs, eleven inches from ceiling back. Well now, Tardigledon, have we thus fucked all our globes? Is all now perfectly iced? The sub-bells' air pine down, did he, rather violent arched, quack it up sufficiently? Where you lead I wish to go, said the shaft, extinguishing all to better taste the white cry. Vexed to death, the furious hole replied: by the mane I drag those untamed ponies galloping o'er graves toward Algabot's red depths! And so forth, the motley sinister and severe shriekings of birds and animals howling from the mappish earth's edge. Pleasure's broth. With pain will you give birth to quaffing tots who'll meet a cruel end. They'll drink the broth of pleasuredice. Their hearts will give birth to other hearts likewise split by hole. Always slipping their bodies 'neath one another, for it's on the sheets, on the sheets, on the sheets, on the sheets and on the mast's flag flapping in funk that their hearts hurl these airs at us from below. Who'll recite for me, head to tail and back of fish, the silly rest of the storyish? Noxious? You hear, Roper? Adramelech from his rung speaks to you with his bread box, he knows his math, can flap, speak Lapp, Adramelech from his rung. Heed me my dear feet, my dear feet heed, this hundredth hoof I lift to the health of boards, i.e., I wish our floors bore not buried us, and bear us erect 'til the end. Sing, faithful legs, plow forth from the plant, survey the terrain! Madame, who dared insult our sufferin' compasses, they are excellent! Each hoof, the price of worthy effort paid, harvests easily at each step nine to 11 inches! Persevere, lower members, persist, by dint of walking again will you in the end obtain premises places countries regions. Gallop always running. Hey there, eyes, I won't let you be sewn shut, got it? And you, come on, quick Adramelech, tell us your memories and views on pig christening, you can do it, your jaws ain't slack! I cannot speak of it. Pigs, pigs! It was Saint Sow's Day, those beasts, fresh from Dagon's hold alive, emaciated its portals, wearing the remains of widows they'd swindled that very morning, melting on our shrouds grown cold, so badly had I bitten them. That they cleft, falling and dashing themselves from the pikes of peaks, while I, coughing and sloughing, rowing and towing, while whereas, from the very heavens pigs greedily christened one another, tasting their blood forming series of sequences of lines of large of troops. All of this in a landscape largely lacking in green. Adramelech, you must now name these beasts. I have forgotten it exactly. One probably bore a name. Guangladeblibardegladon, but 'twas unbeknownst to us, so we called it Behemoth. Addressed it sharply by this name meaning Odette in Hebrew and Leon in Lapp, but not Leon of Abyssinia, the other one, of Greenland. Great clouds clashed in the heavens, emitting brash thunderclaps. A monkey flew a flag on high. A sign at whose sight the bare-assed people waved their hankies. Hankies at whose sight the monkey sang: "'Tis Behemoth, she slinks into the sea with her sisters." Song the people booed. Boo that I, thousandth pedestrian of the name to see at last the piglets' true christening, hooted in the upper half tone. The monkey's fall suggested nothing other than the umpteenth and three hundred sixty-sixth time that a pig more let and better armed flipped the plate beneath my nose. Cup I pick up bent over, unintentionally greeting ass down my life spilled out. In a word, these pretty paper lanterns had blighted my sight. Footless am thus puppet less human face of man turn dead. Tough luck, let's crumble to dust like most. Ouch to my branches, pain to my! Cost the soily sound it launches, cost the soily sound of its drum pound re-sound the devourer's hour! Matter to matter for other livers. That ain't crumbling to dust but sweating out all one's fat. Hoist high the tiny brains! Hey there Lilbit, scratch hard, run thick, quite a few ass isles lay undiscovered! And not much later than just now. February 16th of that year. It was pouring that day. Now I was walking now head down to jump puddles, carefree, caring only to plot my path in mid-center of the street to avoid by habit houses falling on my head. Then shazzam of a sudden and wink of an eye—one thousand phocions!—by chance and in a huge pond's middle I saw my name swim by, its letters floating fleet-like and all afloat. Seafaring dog's wallop! Quick they disappeared, the water awash all again. Quick my head leapt held high instinctively: from the bright white sky fell quick blood drops. They sank quick with no inscription. "Help, here's the rill blood fallin' us, spillin' on our hands!" cried in rapid passing a passerby, sole witness of this dark phenomenon. Then from pointed top of roof, a voice appeared and said: "Abysselech, I centered you, named and selected, I made you. Here is my word, stand and bear it." He named me. And I said: "I don't know how to bear the word, that I am a child, sepulture's sepulture!" He replied: "Do not say I am a child but go to those to whom you will go and say all I order you to." Then he held out his hand to see would I bite and said: "See how I put my words in your mouth." And ever since I've been waiting for my ancient mouth to open, that it may breathe and I speak languages. Yes, yes, my ass, my ass will do the talking, and will smile, and will be magnificent. Just before it disappeared, it added: "Get to it, corporal!" word that opened me from bottom to top. Funereal it appended: "Yack it up, Adramelon!" This latter jab jerked me, and I wept true tears and hiccups. Then it reappeared in other guise, but tiny and then disappeared. It always returns but hid. Troops of elephants, old war lions! Wheels, rascals, vocassian birds, love-struck woodland beasts! Dark fish from deep seas, and you, eluded woodland fools! Bread beasts, lower birds, inhabitants, and lowly birds! Walkers, trotters, cyclists, and inhabitants of woodland deeps! Heavenly and earthly creatures, rush, run, run, run, run, run, run, run, run, run! 'Neath Algabot's slaughter these animals, highly visible and soaked in cold, deprived of their head, dead on their feet and one-eye-blinded by the halo-gasping light of the false sky result only ever from the heaped remains of barrels and know not, so low is the passage, the repeated exodi of their pseudo-procession, the imperial and decisive movement of black plinths' wobbling in fear of splints, and top of it all, the holy sparrow's unwound howling; so unaware are they even today of the popped bottom's great beast, such does it bash below all that covers it up, such the black abyss does hover overhead, such does it flow below all it smashes up. You, all of the all, run from the corner, spin your groups, old vocasson flag holes, assemble that it may ring should that finally triumph in your woodmine ears. Of which local ogler's stupid eye I boot again the stupid gluttonous eye. So that no more 'cept unless widower, to lead us into deceptivity, and so that, so that until this when, so that they may knock onto other hoofs whose instead would stick 'em with radicats of et cetera's exitat albumblition. Well now to this extent, my dear Justin Lorry, gotta reveal your honored of such a day again. Would I not rather talk to the donkey in the field which the thistle grazed lives? Said herbivore inverted. The inveterate bellowed to by-standing milk cows: herd of blunders, beat it! About which not one peep was heard. Was indeed proof that it was worth the trouble, that thanks to the astounding effects of centrifugal force, every thistle's worth its bell! But alas logic got us the opposite. Clandestine Jeremy. It's Adramelech, it's still Adramelech! If Johnny

Fulton, Barton Edmund, and Gallantino, if Bunting Beerbow, Crapton, Dunno, Dandra hear this, then this will be for them! The moment suffices, departure is imminent. Seen and supped already too many of these hatted white figures, pursuing far from above all they hatch to the fine point of fuss incrusture; let them come out or rather let them be click changed into quasi-moons, into ramazons, into the quarter cubes they are! Ugly masks with pierced features, ugly noseless masks, gnawed at masks, farewell say farewell to your eternal dance hall rexecutions, hoist high from the place and exit, or you'll wind up 'neath boolmeeneen, 'neath foolminay quicker'n lickety and sans zigzag! Fake tracks, rapidass shortcuts, faux feet, false messengers, web-footed boxes, painted shafts, false balls and watery footfalls, drop right dead right now! And you true faces, tremble: the times have come to read your features; here, my gimpy finger's poking at your nose. The other the jerk the bird spit up spied the machine thanks to gut. Yes but what advantage? And so forth with all other boats docked at appetite's stopper: The Luzarche, The Pervangel, The Dasher, Val Vertigo, S.S. Savannah. Whose flagged first mate I'm introduced to the captain of the cadets. Three of six kept. Well the tableau's neither beau nor vivant, and nature's poorly rendered, the whole neither done and all detail still to do. For 'gainst a poorly painted background of maritime ocean, an amateur artist with badly split brush (which clearing had already blinded him I doubt it, as for the paralytic we never found out but t'was 15 percent), from behind and before with the frothy-mouthed ship's boy, myself, yes myself, tree'd and speaking to the pilot. And at this speed, it'll fall for sure. Its final effect produced neither comic but unfortunate. In the right corner a cancerous trumpeter hissed the list of my clothes: "Shod in yellow damask leather with laces green, 'neath an oval cap of oak straw beribboned, my hair done up regatta-like, ears hung with pendants, and all arranged to form a block robed in a simple, fetching sheet." And that's all they do they know how to do. Rankin, Lapid, Putter, Hagar, Drury! "Orators are partisans of noise," screamed full steam ahead the canton's paunch. Ah, head-strumpet! Puppet yourself, brandished troglodex's bottle neck, replied without respite alibi's echoes. But we should have said holy avenger, 'cause his very head's executing itself, said a chair 'gainst the wall with a haughty air, poor thing. He, on all fours and already gone from there, opening the door adds: "Still tuned in friends, lift ever lower, member block, your ten cadenced legs, brandished of sound, I hurl high into air your living voices, such is the shallow dance thrown far from the good foot." He's left since that's thrown it. Slipped under the door. Et cetera. And off you go!

Pumpkin on the Air

Michèle Sigal

Translated by Philippa Wehle

CHARACTERS
MAMADOU ROMEO, a Malian
A MALIAN STREET SWEEPER
JULIETTE, eight years old
THE MOTHER
THE FATHER
THE DOCTOR
LOUIS, eight years old
A MALIAN WOMAN
AN UNEMPLOYMENT OFFICE EMPLOYEE

A female passerby, a male passerby, a driver, voices on the radio, newspaper reporters in the street, Chinese workers.

A Parisian street, on a calm morning. Regular sound of a broom sweeping water in the gutter. At first the sound is far off. Then it comes closer and closer.

MAMADOU: Excuse me, madam, I am looking for number 31, Rue de la Liberté.

A FEMALE PASSERBY: 31? 31 ... It's surely between 29 and 33. Did you look? If it's not there, what do you want me do about it?

MAMADOU: Right. ... Excuse me, sir, I'm looking for number 31, Rue de la Liberté.

A Male Passerby *(Talking with his mouth full)*: Rue de la Liberté … Rue de la Liberté … Frankly, that doesn't ring any bells, but I'm not from around here.

Mamadou: La Rue de la Liberté is here, but …

A Male Passerby: Hey there, are you pulling my leg or what? *(He wrinkles up a paper wrapping and throws it on the ground.)*

Mamadou: … I know the street, but number 31? *(He says a few words in Malian.)* 25, 27, 29 … 33, 35, 37 …

A Street Sweeper *(Has come up to where Mamadou is standing. He speaks to him in Malian)*: Are you looking for something?

Mamadou: How do you know I'm from Mali?

A Street Sweeper: From the way you're squinting at reality.

Mamadou: I may be squinting, but you, you've got a beautiful broom! I came to France to look for one just like that. My cousin wrote me to come to his house. He said he lives at 31, Rue de la Liberté.

A Street Sweeper *(In Malian)*: Well, here it is.

Mamadou: This crumbling wall? These boarded-up windows? And this bricked-up door? You want me to believe that's where my cousin lives?

A Street Sweeper: Used to live.

Mamadou *(Starts out in Malian)*: Do you mean to say I crossed the ocean crouched down in the hold, my stomach all twisted with fear that I'd be discovered and thrown overboard. I left my sunshine and my friends, risked my life and held on to my dream surrounded by sharks … *(He finishes in Malian.)* … just to end up in front of a blank wall?

A Street Sweeper: If you want a broom like mine, here's the address where you can get one. It's the town hall. You can't miss it. It's really big and really ugly, unless my eyes have deceived me.

Mamadou: Are you sure it's not all boarded up there as well?

A Street Sweeper: Well, if it is, you'll just have to go back to Mali. *(He moves away as he sweeps the gutter.)* The subway's at the corner, near the newspaper stand. You'll find another cousin there to show you the way. Let your eyes speak to you. Listen to them.

Mamadou: Meanwhile an elephant is coming out of the newspaper stand. It's wearing Africa on its back and has two brooms to defend itself with. The pachyderm crosses the area dreaming its nonchalant dream which makes the pavement shake. *(Trumpeting.)* Hey! Wait for me! Do you know where I can find my cousin? *(Sound of screeching brakes.)*

A Driver: So, what's the crosswalk for, dogs?

Mamadou: There's a guy who doesn't know how to look where he's going. These Parisians. Just put them behind a wheel and they lose control and can't tell a dog from a Malian. Brrr, it's really cold here! *(A few words in Malian.)* "I've never been so cold in my life!" *(Dissolve to Juliette's voice, heard reading a story.)*

Juliette: "After a full day, as he was returning to his palace, the King had an accident on the Expressway. The shock was so violent that the taxi was reduced to pulp the size of a pumpkin. The King thought he was already dead when he clearly heard the weather report for the coming days: 'Occasional light rain and periods of sun here and there, etc …' He realized he was still alive and so was his car radio."

The Mother: Juliette, you have to go to bed. You've got school tomorrow.

Juliette *(Yawning)*: "While help was taking forever to come, he listened to his radio in his pulp of a pumpkin …"

Background sounds of the radio. Frequent changing of stations. A faucet is dripping. Every now and again, THE FATHER clears his throat.

FATHER: Juliette, study your multiplication tables instead of dreaming.

JULIETTE: Ever since my father, an unemployed taxi driver, has been out of work, his car is just a memory that he places on the kitchen table and listens to with his head in his hands so he can remember the happy times when he used to drive his taxi from dusk to dawn. His car radio is the apple of his eye, his very own pumpkin, his most treasured possession. Sometimes with the wave of a magic wand, it turns back into a taxi ... *(A female broadcaster's voice announces traffic jams along the banks of the Seine.)* The voices of sirens beckon him to the banks of the Seine, the unknown soldier's flame waves to him Place de l'Etoile, and the Statue of the Republic sings loudly to him from her throne. Sitting in the middle of nowhere, bewitched by these disembodied voices, the King sets sail and goes off in search of his lost kingdom. *(The dripping water is becoming increasingly loud.)* As for me, I'm doing my homework paddling along side him on a little paper raft and I drown in my multiplication tables right under his nose. *(Sound of keys in the door.)*

THE MOTHER: What's all this water? Is there a leak or something? You forgot to shut off the faucet again. I get home as late as possible so I can avoid the traffic and you bring it home. Please turn off that radio or I'll throw it out the window. *(THE FATHER clears his throat as if he were coming out of a deep sleep and was going to say something.)* Eight o'clock and I still have to get caught in the middle of traffic before making dinner.

JULIETTE: He thinks she won't do it, that it's a refrain in a song without any rimes.

THE MOTHER: So you think I won't do it?

JULIETTE: Still with all that anger, you never know. So he cuts the only thread that connects him to his former kingdom, and a huge silence, as sudden as an air pocket, fills the apartment as if Gulliver or an elephant or the owner just came in. I hang on to my multiplication tables so I won't fall in, but …

The Mother: When this radio is gone, you'll have to face life.

Juliette: That's just it. Life makes him sick to his stomach. Whenever he looks at reality, it breaks like a windshield into a thousand pieces that cut him and dance before his crazed eyes like butterflies in the light. So he closes his eyes. *(Long dizzying silence that becomes the fluttering of butterfly wings.)*

The Doctor: Now see here, we'll never get anywhere this way. Help me if you want us to take a few baby steps towards a cure. Say something that will get us started on our way.

The Father *(The fluttering becomes more intense every time he is seized with anguish)*: Butterflies.

The Doctor: Butterflies! You too? I've always had a passion for butterflies! The Borbo Borbonica, the Plantan Blue, the purple Hesperides and even the little firey one. What a wonderful world! Unfortunately, you don't see many of them anymore, what with all the pollution. *(He begins leafing through a medical dictionary.)*

The Father: Oh I see thousands of them! They flutter up to the tops of the high pine trees and carry me off on the whirlwind of their dizzying nuptial flight. Imagine, Doctor, thousands of butterflies in love fluttering around in a meadow bathed in the rays of a radiant sun …

The Doctor: A meadow, in the city?

The Father: After hours of amorous display, they'd fall on the windshield and die from exhaustion. I'd feel dizzy. I always drove my taxi with my eyes closed, without any map, but ever since I lost my job, I feel like a stranger in my own city. Not to mention that I feel like I'm bothering them while they're in the middle of mating.

The Doctor: Your clients?

The Father: No, the butterflies.

The Doctor: I see, I see ... Butterflies, butterflies ... *(Fluttering of butterfly wings.)* An interesting case, but this dictionary is 25 years behind the times! It describes work-related pathologies that no longer exist, while unemployment-related illnesses that are on the upswing are completely ignored. There's almost an epidemic in the city. A huge continent, a numerical wasteland, when in fact there're enough jobs for the next ten years. *(He is still leafing through the medical dictionary.)*

The Father: My life's in trouble and I'm seeing double not to mention my ocular migrations and circulation problems. It's a real nightmare! It's hard to find work under these circumstances, especially as a taxi driver.

The fluttering of wings moves away and it seems quite clear that there's an insect hitting the windowpanes.

The Doctor: Unemployment is the future of medicine. If only we had a good dictionary. Ah! Butterfly ... See chrysalid. "Chrysalid syndrome. Appears after a violent shock. The sick person retreats into a cocoon and refuses to come out." Where did you go?

The Father: Behind you, Doctor.

The Doctor *(Stuttering from surprise)*: What are you doing so close to the window?

The Father: It's nothing, Doctor, a dizzy spell, a shower of light, an irresistible urge to bang my head against the pane.

The Doctor: You're going to break it! Open the window! "Prescribed treatment: wait for the counter shock or bring it on." When did your circular migrations first occur?

The Father: Exactly one month ago.

The Doctor: Right after the terrible accident that totaled your taxi? According to the garage mechanic's autopsy, you should be dead. "Sides all bent in, gas tank burned up, thorasic cage caved in, dashboard all chewed up, traumatism in the rear …"

The Father: Miraculously I survived but my life is hell. It's filled with lepidopterae!

The Doctor: Depression of the unemployed, feelings of guilt toward the one who fed you and whose life you couldn't save. Wait until it all backfires and come back to see me in six months after you've finished the migratory treatment. Don't be so impatient. I'll open the window for you.

The butterflies fly away. Street noises. Juliette is playing hopscotch on the sidewalk. Louis, the owner's son, arrives at full speed on his skates.

Louis: Get out of my way. I don't have any brakes.

Juliette: Are you skating on my hopscotch board on purpose?

Louis: You gotta be kidding, I can't stop …

Juliette: The sidewalk's for pedestrians.

Louis: So go to Mars if you don't like it.

Juliette: It's my street.

Louis: Ah!!!! *(He crashes violently into the garbage cans.)* Your street really stinks. Don't the garbage collectors ever come by here?

Juliette: Garbage cans don't smell very good. They're made to contain bad odors.

Louis: Smells like dead cat.

Juliette: Rotten eggs.

Louis: Like shit.

Juliette: Like something burning.

Louis: Spoiled meat.

A sort of sung lament rises up from the garbage. From now on, the two youngsters lower their voices.

Juliette: A talking garbage can!

Louis: People will throw anything in them.

Juliette: Help me get him out of there. *(She tries to set the garbage can upright.)*

Louis: You gotta be kidding! Maybe he's been in the garbage can a long time. He must be half rotten. You can't understand what he's saying.

Juliette: If he was rotten, he wouldn't be talking. Maybe he's hurt.

Louis: I'm getting out of here. I don't want to catch tetanus. *(He runs off.)*

Mamadou *(In Malian and then in French)*: The elephant ran away and took Africa with it. I'm cold. I don't know this country, this city, this climate.

Juliette: You're alive?

Mamadou: I was so happy in the forest. The moon was dancing among the tree tops and the grass smelled so sweet … *(He coughs.)* Who are you? Why did you wake me up? Let me go back in there. *(Garbage can noises.)*

JULIETTE: It's not a forest. It's a garbage can.

MAMADOU: What are you saying? I'm not quite awake yet but still. *(In Malian then in French.)* Ever since I got to Paris, my mind's all foggy. *(He coughs.)* My broom, where's my broom? Oh thank God I didn't lose it. It was a very expensive broom. It's the reason I came all this way here. I made a trip to the land of garbage cans. That makes you laugh?

JULIETTE: I'd have nightmares if I slept in the street.

MAMADOU: Me too. What's your name?

JULIETTE: Juliette.

MAMADOU: Hello Juliette. I'm Romeo.

JULIETTE: Romeo? *(They laugh.)*

MAMADOU: Yes. You see, chance brought us both to the same sidewalk, but not to the same continent. I came to France to work and take care of my family back in Mali, but I've never dreamed of Africa as much as since I got to Paris. I'm looking for my cousin who's supposed to give me a place to stay. Meanwhile, I've been sleeping out in the open. Though there's not much in the way of open sky around here. *(He coughs.)*

JULIETTE: It must get cold at night.

MAMADOU: Cold as blazes. *(He coughs.)* I never start my day without asking myself about my health. How you doing? I ask myself, to get warm. "How are you this morning, Mamadou? Did you sleep well?"

JULIETTE: Isn't your name Romeo?

MAMADOU *(Drums softly on a garbage can lid, like a storyteller accompanying himself with a tamborine)*: Yes it is. Mamadou Romeo. "Did you have sweet dreams, Mamadou Romeo? Probably a few aches and pains?" "No. Not a single one. I feel fresh and ready to go and in a very good mood." "And how about your intestines, not too messed up?" "Um ..." "Are you sure you digested your food well? Mamadou Romeo Bankalé? With what you had for dinner, that would be surprising!" "That's true, very surprising but I assure you ..." "Don't lie, Mamadou Romeo Bankalé Baba, there was a storm last night and you're soaked to the bone." "Really, I hadn't noticed. Still it's true. I am wet." *(Coughs.)* "Don't tell me you're planning to dry off in the sun of the Eiffel Tower, Mamadou Romeo Bankalé Baba Baracouna. Don't tell me that." "But if I don't say anything, I'll die from the cold! Let me talk. You know that words warm you up." "Lies warm you less than a fire made out of straw, Mamadou Romeo Bankalé Baba, fabricator and liar on top of that." "Don't be so mean to me!" *(He repeats in Malian.)* "Don't be so mean to me." *(Coughs.)* "I'm very careful not to lie, I assure you, but sometimes my tongue plays tricks on me and the truth trips and hurts me." *(The drumming stops. He coughs.)* That's how I start every day of my new life, sweeping away the lies that keep me warm at night.

JULIETTE: They aren't lies if you tell them to yourself.

MAMADOU: The biggest lies are the ones we tell ourselves. They carry us off into a story that isn't our own, and all we have left is the subway stations to help us find our way in life. In a word, I wash myself with good soap every morning. I rub myself hard to start off the day and chase away the illusions and the smells of warm croissants. *(Trumpeting.)* Hush, animal, it's not time yet. I'm talking to Juliette and you're only a dream. *(He says a few words in Malian and imitates the song of an exotic bird.)* I've made three wishes. I've only got two left.

THE MOTHER: Juliette! Come eat!

MAMADOU: Go. They're calling you.

JULIETTE: I want to hear the rest.

MAMADOU: Do you have a balcony?

JULIETTE: No.

MAMADOU: That's okay. When you get home, I'll send you a hummingbird. He'll tell you the story of the broom that returns to the forest after a long absence.

He chirps like a bird while sweeping the gutter. Dissolve into the next sequence. We hear the sounds of forks as well as the news on the radio.

THE MOTHER: Are you swallowing the flies or eating your spinach? Turn down the radio. She's listening and it keeps her from eating.

JULIETTE: I'm listening to the bird.

THE FATHER: The sparrows make so much noise that I have to turn the radio up.

JULIETTE: It's not a sparrow. It's a hummingbird.

THE MOTHER: The only birds in Paris are swallows and pigeons.

THE FATHER: It's coming from the Chinese workroom. They like birds to keep them company.

THE MOTHER: I doubt that with all the precautions they take so nobody will notice them. They come and go without opening any doors and they manage to sew without anybody hearing the noise from their machines, even at night. So they're sure not going to wake up the neighborhood with the sounds of birds.

THE FATHER: What if they're homesick? If it lets them increase their productivity while decreasing their nostalgia, that's all to the good.

THE MOTHER: Anyway they don't bother anybody. They don't make any noise. It's as if we dreamed them up. Perfect neighbors.

The bird songs become chirps, and the chirps get louder as if we were in a large birdcage. THE FATHER *turns up the radio accordingly and the voices get louder. The Monza Automobile Race Prize is being rebroadcast on the news.*

THE FATHER: I don't know if those are real Chinese people, but I'm sure those are fake birds. It's a recording.

THE MOTHER: Maybe it's a workroom with a hidden room: legal birds, in front, illegal workers, without papers, in back. That way, if the police come, they'll get a free concert.

JULIETTE: I'd really like to have a concert of birds in the forest for Christmas.

THE FATHER: I hear the Americans are really good at that. They even record traffic noises on their highways and then they listen to them in their dining rooms, at the office, at the Mickey D's, and even in their cars. It seems it relaxes them. It's Zen and it takes away their aggression. It's wonderful! The problem is it also erases their brains.

THE MOTHER: We're always behind in France.

A news flash interrupts the programs. The bird calls have stopped. The family has stopped talking. The radio screams in the middle of dead silence, before the father turns the radio down. In the street, MAMADOU *lets out a long lament in Malian as* JULIETTE *runs to the window.*

THE RADIO: A fire has broken out in a rundown building occupied by some African families. Seventeen dead, 14 of them children. This tragedy reminds us once again of the disturbing and infuriating living conditions of poor people and immigrants. It was the second fire in four days, and it reveals the conditions in which numerous immigrants live, without water or electricity, in an overcrowded dirty room. Many of them have been waiting for decent housing for years.

MAMADOU: *(A long lament in Malian.)*

Juliette: Romeo!

The Mother: Juliette! Your spinach.

Juliette *(To herself)*: What is Popeye doing in this story? Romeo! Romeo. I want to hear the ending even if it is sad. Don't pay any attention to what my mother's saying. She still thinks I'm four years old.

The Radio: Now suffering has been added to their poverty. No government has really dealt with housing problems. *(The Father turns off the radio. We hear footsteps in the street at night.)*

Mamadou *(Sniffs, breathes in the air, and moves toward the smell)*: It's over here. It smells like mechoui. What a bummer, cousin. Just when I've found you, you go up in smoke. Where are you now? Can you hear me, cousin? It's me, Mamadou Romeo Bankalé Baba Baracouna, liar and on occasion teller of tall tales, but I swear to you on my mother's head, I'm not joking tonight.

A Woman *(In Malian)*: Who are you talking to, and what are you doing snooping around in these ruins?

Mamadou: Ah!!! Mama, what are you doing here? Has someone cast a spell on me?

A Woman: I don't know what mother gave birth to this idiot, but thank God it wasn't me. I came to pick up some things and I'm very angry.

Mamadou: Have you gone to live with misfortune, cousin, or does it move around with you every time?

A Woman: Open your eyes once and for all and you'll see that I'm not your cousin. And where do you see any misfortune? All I see is injustice. I have a job. I pay my taxes just like the French do, but I live in a slum. What do you think? That they're going to put you in a low-income housing palace because you sweep the streets of Paris? After every fire, you can smell burnt black flesh for two or three days and then the wind smothers the shouts and scatters the ashes and promises. So there, I'm done. That's all that's left of my belongings, barely enough to fill a bag from the Monoprix. *(She moves away.)* As for your cousin, I don't know, go see at the Quatre Chemins hotel at the Aubervilliers gate. Next time, come sooner.

He thanks her in Malian and she wishes him good luck in Malian.

MAMADOU: The subway at night time is a bit like Bamako. It's warm. There are benches where you can lie down and dream for very little money. A round trip to California for the price of a life in Mali. That's a fine ad. It says so. One night, when I was traveling around the world in this dream set, I saw an elephant go by. He went through the turnstile as if it were nothing, with Africa on its back and just one token. It was a bit much, but nobody said anything. I was so tired that I just let my dream come unglued. Without that backdrop, I walked all night long like a zombie. Only one of my three wishes is left.

Trumpeting and closing of the automatic subway gates. The last subway disappears into the tunnel. MAMADOU is sleeping on a bench in front of the Quatre Chemins hotel. It is dawn. Day is beginning to break, but a fire is starting up in one of the hotel rooms. It's spitting, softly at first, a few voices waking up, then sudden panic: smoke, coughing, shouts, calling out in different African languages, general confusion, sirens. These sounds grow louder and louder throughout MAMADOU's monologue.

MAMADOU: "Hey, Mamadou! Wake up!" "Ah … let me sleep!" "It's not a good time." "Um …" "Wake up. You're not in California any more." "Ah …" "Can't you hear that little spitting sound?" "Ah … ah." "Can't you smell that burning smell?" "Leave me be. I'm tired!" "I thought you wanted to get here before the fire?" *(MAMADOU bolts up, suddenly awake.)* "What fire?" "Oh now you want to know! "What's happening?" "Get up from your bench, lazybones, get out of here." "Calm down, calm down, don't confuse me, please. I don't want to miss my last chance to find my cousin." "You've lost your mind, Mamadou Romeo, with your look of a real fake sweeper, you're perfect to get yourself carted off as a prime suspect." "Why's that? I haven't done anything." *(He bursts out laughing.)* "You want people to believe you, a big fellow with frizzy hair like you? You're not going to become as white as snow in five minutes when you're black from head to toe, worse than a piece of coal." *(Annoyed.)* "I'm waiting for my cousin." "Naïve Mamadou, run like Hell and get out of here, Romeo, and take all your names with you so no one can ever find you." "I can't. I made a wish." "What's that all about? All you're going to get is to smell like a roasted black man." "It's my last chance." "You'll have other opportunities. The season's just begun. It's not that I want you to rush, but Paris is burning brighter than the fires in the African brush. Next time, be more careful. Don't get here before the disaster." "Do you think I planned it? ... " *(Police sirens.)* "I don't think anything. Now scram!" *(MAMADOU runs off. The fire moves away. We only hear MAMADOU's breathing and his blood beating in his temples. Trumpeting.)* It's over there, at the crossroads. It's carrying Africa on its back and it's following its flimsy dream. Up I go! I hoist myself up, grab hold and hang on with all my might, but Africa could care less about me. She's not about to give up the slightest bit of life to me, "Move over, you careless fellow. You're in my way. You're suffocating me. You're strangling me," she says to me. "But I'm not crazy. I don't want to strangle my country." *(A silent struggle ensues. All you can hear is MAMADOU's breathing combined with the static on the radio.)*

THE RADIO: A new fire has broken out in a hotel in Aubervilliers where Malian families have been living while waiting for housing. They are legal immigrants. They have money, but they've never received a positive answer to their requests for housing.

MAMADOU: "Don't insist, Mamadou. I was here before you. You can see there's only room for one of us." "Who do you think you are, Africa?" "Let me go, Mamadou Romeo Bankalé, or you'll be sorry ... " "You're the one who's holding on to me." "Get off of me, you parasite!" *(MAMADOU and Africa fall down. Trumpeting and long lament in Malian.)* "You can get up, Mamadou, but if you want to pursue your African dream, you'll have to do it alone and with an elephant on your back."

The window is open. Regular sound of a broom in the gutter water. The radio stays on low throughout the meal. A few words grasped here and there make it clear that the broadcast concerns the terrible conditions under which certain families have to live.

JULIETTE *(Runs to the window)*: "Romeo!"

THE MOTHER: Don't lean out that way! That balcony's too rickety!

JULIETTE: "Romeo!" It's not him.

THE MOTHER: That's all we need!

THE FATHER: So they're studying Shakespeare in elementary school now?

JULIETTE: It's Louis. He has lots of Shakespeare videos.

THE MOTHER: And why not porno tapes as well? I forbid you to play with the owner's son!

JULIETTE: You're the one who told me to …

THE FATHER: Listen, Juliette, it's a matter of … how much … Those people have lost all sense of relativity. That's normal when your bathroom is the size of a three-room apartment, but when families with 15 children who pile into a bathroom that measures three-by-six feet, it's an upside-down world.

JULIETTE: I don't see the connection to Shakespeare.

THE FATHER *(Clearing his throat)*: It's not as romantic but you'll understand later on.

THE MOTHER: While you're waiting, eat your spaghetti.

JULIETTE *(To herself)*: Romeo has disappeared. No news of the hummingbird. They got lost on the way when they took the subway to go back to Bamako. Fortunately Romeo is clever. He dropped golden corn seeds that shine in the moonlight …

THE MOTHER: Can't you see she's got her head in the clouds and she isn't eating because of the radio? Some day she's going to disappear and I'll have told you so.

JULIETTE *(To herself)*: Who me? Eating spaghetti with Bolognaise sauce isn't going to make me transparent. *(A door slams.)* Irritated, the King takes his kingdom into the next room because the Queen can no longer tolerate a husband without a throne. And to top it all off, they only have one daughter and that's me. The Queen can't stand it any longer. The Queen is at the end of her rope. If only she'd go cry in the garden, I'd make the spaghetti disappear from my story and go off looking for Romeo.

A door slams in the Unemployment Office. An EMPLOYEE *is stapling files.*

THE EMPLOYEE: Close the door. You're letting a draft in. And stop fluttering around like a butterfly. You're making me dizzy.

THE FATHER *(To himself)*: She stapled me. She's going to give me the third degree, that's for sure. She's preparing her interrogation before she nails me with two or three pointed questions.

THE EMPLOYEE: Sit down. I'm not going to eat you. You've been unemployed since …

THE FATHER *(Clearing his throat. Muted fluttering of butterfly wings)*: Six months.

THE EMPLOYEE: You're really lucky. We've already found you a job: force feeding geese, in Mont-de-Marsan, in the Landes region.

The Father *(Fluttering of wings and screeching of a chair on the ground)*: But I'm a taxi driver in Paris.

The Employee: I know how to read, but while you're waiting. You start Monday.

The Father *(To himself)*: I've been feeling better for some time now. I didn't have those butterflies in front of my eyes and now my eye migrations are starting up again.

The Employee *(Stapling files together)*: You're really lucky. You're going to inaugurate the new law that supports those who are willing to move somewhere else. Please fill out this questionnaire. Just the first 15 pages.

The Father *(To himself)*: How am I going to change into a butterfly in Mont-de-Marsan when my cocoon is in Paris?

The Employee: You've got all weekend to move.

The Father *(To himself)*: If the butterflies are going to multiply at the speed of the men out of work, it doesn't leave me any time to rest. I'm caught in an infernal spiral I … I … *(Fluttering of butterflies taking off.)*

The Employee: Where is he? Really! Where are you? *(Doors slam.)* We find them work and all the thanks we get is a door slammed in our faces. Next!

She tears up the file. Dissolve to The Father listening to a radio broadcast about unemployment. Juliette is doing her homework. The Mother is back from her job.

The Radio: Unemployment figures have reached 1,239,000 as compared to 1,219,000 during the second trimester last year, which amounts to an increase of 1.6 percent, coming from the rural areas alone….

Juliette: Poor papa. He's so depressed by the war! He thinks that's he's fought the good fight but the next day he finds out on the radio that the enemy has gained ground.

THE MOTHER: So, what happened at the Unemployment Office?

THE FATHER *(Sneezing and muttering)*: Mont-de-Marsan, in the Landes, where the Douze River meets the Midou, 29,489 inhabitants, 30 tons of goose liver a year …

THE MOTHER: Turn down the radio. I can't hear what you're saying.

JULIETTE: But my baba caught code in the Unembloyment Office where the angry boors are chattering.

THE MOTHER: Every time you come back from the Unemployment Office, you're in a bad mood. Turn that radio off before I throw it out the window.

JULIETTE: The apple of his eye, the music of his life.

THE FATHER *(The program about unemployment continues. He turns up the volume)*: When you've almost died, you really care about proof that you exist.

THE MOTHER *(Her voice rising)*: You're going to have to live without proof one of these days!

JULIETTE: His miracle, his oracle, his Holy Virgin, his pumpkin.

THE MOTHER: Okay. You asked for it! *(She opens the window and throws the radio out.)*

JULIETTE: Oh, no! Mother!

Silence. Then the glass roof of the workroom shatters. Silence, followed by violent explosions, followed by a thundering "Cock-a-doodle-doo" and much confusion. Voices shouting, calling out in Chinese, followed by sentence fragments from the reporters' voices.

Reporters' Voices: "Cock-a-doodle-doo!"

Sentence fragments in Chinese.

The last day of the last lunar month on the Chinese calendar …

We still don't know if there are any victims from the radio but it did cause quite a bit of damage …

"Cock-a-doodle-doo!"

Sentence fragments in Chinese.

Juliette: After a soaring flight, the radio fell on the workroom's glass roof where authentic Chinese people were manufacturing real firecrackers and sewing real dragons for their Chinese New Year celebration.

Reporters' Voices: *(Sentence fragments in Chinese.)*

This workroom employed some twenty clandestine workers, from China, working like slaves …

Sentence fragments in Chinese.

It must be said that it is the year 4703 on the Chinese calendar …

"Cock-a-doodle-doo!"

The Year of the Rooster …

"Cock-a-doodle-doo! Cock-a-doodle-doo!"

A missile, fallen from the sky …

No path will be left unturned …

Sentence fragments in Chinese.

JULIETTE: Shocked into reality, the radio exploded and my father ran to the balcony. He couldn't believe his eyes. No more dizzy spells. No more butterflies.

REPORTERS' VOICES: Due to the shock, the Year of the Rooster has begun six months ahead of time, leaving the Chinese community in a state of great disarray....

Sentence fragments in Chinese.

Working conditions are deplorable, inhuman....

Sentence fragments in Chinese.

The sewing machines were in the basement....

Sentence fragments in Chinese.

It was also used as a storage space. ... A whole arsenal needed to celebrate the Chinese New Year.

The sound of a firecracker followed by: "Cock-a-doodle-doo!"

The Chinese love firecrackers ...

The Year of the Rooster was supposed to start off under the best of conditions....

For the astrologers ...

The Chinese love them ...

Some were found three floors down in the basement, no legal papers or housing....

A sign from heaven!

No path will be left unturned....

Sentence fragments in Chinese.

JULIETTE: When he found the remains of his radio lying on the ground in the middle of lanterns and dragons, my father didn't cry. He opened his eyes wide so he could look directly at a world he didn't know, a world that was there, nearby, right below him, at his feet.

REPORTERS' VOICES: *(Sentence fragments in Chinese. The sound of a firecracker followed by: "Cock-a-doodle-doo!")*

The Minister of the Interior ...

Sentence fragments in Chinese.

The rooster, a symbol of energetic strength, rigor and passion ...

All fired up, as always, the Minister of Calamity was the first to arrive at the site of insanity where he declared war on the fire. ... *(Firecrackers.)*

"Cock-a-doodle-doo!" "Cock-a-doodle-doo!"

The Chinese appreciate his leadership qualities, his sense of organization, his rare strength of character, his great efficiency at work...

The New Year begins full of promise six months ahead of time...

"Cock-a-doodle-doo!" "Cock-a-doodle-doo!" "Cock-a-doodle-doo!"

A door slams.

JULIETTE: Papa! *(Silence.)* He took his coat, put on his hat, went out to take a walk into life, and was cured.

Inventories

Philippe Minyana

Translated by Philippa Wehle

AUTHOR'S NOTE

This could be a sort of "game show": a talking marathon: the object is to tell one's life story, to tell everything…

There are different sound and light cues that let the contestants know when it is their turn. (These interrupt them as well.)

Stage front: a sort of garland of lights arranged in a semi-circle to define a space to encompass their words. (The contestants introduce themselves in the beginning of the show.)

There are also three stools.

The female moderator, Eve, could also be a male moderator. Her comments could be longer: improvisation on the idea of a television or radio show….

CHARACTERS

Jacqueline, a contestant
Angele, a contestant
Barbara, a contestant
Eve, a female moderator
Igor, a male moderator (offstage; voice heard over a microphone)

Eve comes out and introduces herself to the audience.

Eve: Hello, my name is Eve. Tonight our guests are Jacqueline, Angèle, and Barbara … I'll go get them! *(She goes toward the wings. To the contestants:)* You can come in! *(The three contestants come in. Eve calls them over to the microphone.)* Jacqueline Mettetal! Angèle Rougeot! Barbara Fesselet!

The three contestants come forward with their treasured objects: Jacqueline carries a washbasin in her hand, Barbara has a lamp stand, and Angèle is wearing a dress from 1954.

Eve: Jacqueline Mettetal!

Jacqueline *(Speaks to the audience)*: Hello! I'm really afraid to talk to you about my washbasin because it goes so far back and when I go far back like that it stirs up layers and layers of feeling and if you touch those layers it'd be better not to touch them and I'm stupidly smiling like this with my mouth wide open because I'm uncomfortable I feel it in my stomach a knot in the stomach Alka Seltzer's not going to make it go away and telling you about my washbasin might just make my knot worse since the basin is tied to stories that aren't very funny I often laugh when I don't really feel like laughing I'm good at pretending I've had a rough time of it I have to say my washbasin's my whole life it's just a basin but sometimes it's the basins that tell your life story best I can already tell you that I don't like the Southern Turnpike my guys and I we'd go south every chance we got and when I see the Southern Turnpike exit ramp it reminds me of my guys and I don't have any guys anymore so the south forget it! No I'm not going to tell you about my basin after all see I'm not smiling anymore I feel more like bursting into tears! I had three kids and then one night … Oh boy there's that damn knot again and I'm smiling with my big mouth wide open that must look like quite a face and everybody tells me: why do you smile like that Jacqueline what with the life you've had!

Eve: Thank you! Angèle Rougeot!

Angèle *(Wearing a dress from the 50s, she speaks to the audience)*: Hello! Don't be surprised if I raise my eyebrows a lot it's not a twitch or maybe it is a twitch! When I was very young I'd pluck my eyebrows and raise them up high like this like certain artists do the ones who raise their eyebrows up high I realized that every time they raised them it was in love scenes and right after the eyebrow thing there'd be the kissing thing! I was very very naïve and I went on plucking my eyebrows and raising them up higher and higher I'd even add some with a pencil the more my private life went downhill the more I'd pluck them and the more I'd raise them up my son who's in theater told me: Mother, stop doing that with your eyebrows I almost stopped but when you've raised your eyebrows so high for such a long time it's hard not to raise them at all! I still raise them from time to time when I'm a little embarrassed I'm really embarrassed now I've got really bad circulation my hands are swollen my feet too I wonder if I've always called attention to my eyebrows so people wouldn't notice my hands my circulation's been bad for a really long time I've got tons of problems with circulation and I wore my dress from 1954 I'm ridiculous, aren't I? Sure I am ... There's one thing that has really mattered to me and that's my 1954 dress the dress the shoes the bag too but I'm only going to talk about the dress actually these shoes this bag aren't from 54 someone lent them to me the real ones are shot! I'm going to try to stop doing the eyebrow thing but a muscle must have gotten used to it so it does whatever it likes still I've played a lot of sports swimming but you can't control everything my legs my arms they're okay no problem I'm not ashamed of my breasts and I'm a grandmother! My mother's dead so are my father and my husband almost no sisters the youngest yes but she's in Guadeloupe my cousins, uncles, aunts all dead! But I've kept everything knick knacks mementos junk I've got cookies from Canet pine cones from the Sainte-Maxime camping grounds, this dress oh dear oh dear!

Eve: Thank you! Barbara Fesselet!

Barbara *(Holding a lamp stand in her hands, she speaks to the audience)*: Hello I'm very happy to be here my life's such a desert this piece of junk's really heavy! I could have brought a chain bracelet or a vase but I chose a lamp it's my number one treasure right you know my life by heart! I've got a postcard collection but Brittany, Switzerland, the Jura mountains, the Côte d'Azur I've got a postcard from Mexico I always say that this lamp and my dog are essential to me oh when my dog dies my life's been filled with dogs I adore cats! I'm limping a little this evening it's not going to last I've always loved dancing I listen to the radio and I dance yesterday I danced and wham I shouldn't have still I work out on a stationary bike in my bedroom I open the window and voilà! an inside courtyard in the 18th district it's not the country but you have to take care of your body I never stop thinking about that I've also got photographs of all of my nephews on my sideboard Christophe Guillaume Auguste Auguste poor guy but nobody here knows them! Do you see what I'm doing? My hands get all tense and I dig my nails into the palms it's pretty painful it's a side effect of my anxiety what have I got at home that really matters to me? A tablecloth maybe yes a 19th-century tablecloth I take calcium and iron homeopathic remedies but my hands still get all tense my grandmother did the same thing I've got my father's nose my mother's hair I've also got pictures of my parents in frames with elaborate silver designs on them it's the frames I like in museums the paintings too but we've seen reproductions of them and the colors aren't the same hey big guy say hello to these nice ladies and gentlemen: it's sending you a kiss! The story of the lamp is the heart of my story so we can start with the lamp.

EVE: Thank you! Jacqueline Mettetal!

JACQUELINE *(Speaking to the audience)*: I live on Girardot Street in Bagnolet Girardot was the guy who invented peaches I work at the town hall! I've had eight kids with two guys seven with the same guy one with the other! I got rid of my last guy right away the first one lasted longer fifteen years! I had a hard time getting over that beautiful love story fifteen years of happiness he invented Gaston the Borneo monkey for the kids he loved our kids he was a painter we'd spend entire days at the Louvre I'd dream about success not about being rich! I got rid of a lot of things because I don't want them anymore: furniture letters! Photographs … But not this one! That's me! OK, so I'm going to tell you the story of the washbasin here I go it reminds me of the first time I rode a moped!

Eve: We'll get to that later! Thank you! Angèle Rougeot!

Angèle *(Speaking to the audience)*: This is the 1954 dress. These are the 54 shoes. This is the 54 bag. Everything's 54. My son's an intellectual he's in the theatre he's the love of my life there are so many children who die in the Philippines fortunately liver transplants give us hope I feel bad for the Arabs and all immigrants and what can be done to save the forests nothing! And everybody's dying dying dying Simone de Beauvoir Simone Signoret François Truffaut Danny Kaye Romy Schneider Jean Gabin Brejnev Johnny Weismuller ...

Jacqueline: Jean-Paul Sartre!

Angèle: Jean-Paul Sartre Orson Welles Jacques Tati Dalida Rita Hayworth Grace Kelly and it's not over yet! And when's the Third World War going to happen! I kept Papa's cuckoo clock because it's a lovely cuckoo clock.

Eve: Thank you! Barbara!

Barbara *(Speaking to the audience)*: I have three idols: Ivan the Terrible Blue Beard Peter the Great and I don't want to die before finding another Chinese man I adore the Chinese I'm divorced no children I live on Poulet Street I make love with some of my colleagues but I don't kiss them they take me from behind I prefer that position so I don't have to kiss them! They all want to kiss me I don't want them to kiss me I prefer the North Sea my dog is 17 years old I hate my apartment I watch TV the other day a young man wanted to kiss me I told him: get the hell out of here I hate hypocrisy I say everything I think I forgive stupidity not meanness it's hard living alone as someone said, "Somewhere there must be a man who's right for you," I haven't found him yet he must exist maybe I'll never meet you I adore Portugal I adore this necklace!

Eve: Thank you! Barbara thank you thank you very much. Ladies, go over there underneath your photographs! *(The contestants take their places under their pictures.)* So when the lights go up you're going to rush over to sit down quick quick quick and then it's your turn to talk. Attention! ... Attention ... Attention ...

A stool is placed at the rear of the stage. Three flex-stem lamps with blue bulbs on them are placed stage front along with three horns. The lights are focused on the three photographs of the contestants. The game begins. Light on ANGÈLE's horn. ANGÈLE runs to the stool and starts to talk. The other two will do the same.

ANGÈLE: This is the 1954 dress the destiny dress let's call it the love dress this dress is Marcel I was married to Abel but there was Marcel I lied to Abel because I loved Marcel one morning I went to the Electricity Company it was June 5, 1954, and he said to me: what are you doing for lunch? I was living on the Rue du Chemin Vert the Electricity Company's on the Rue de Bagnolet I said my food's waiting for me at home and he said: let's go to a restaurant ... *(A noise interrupts her. Light on BARBARA's horn.)*

BARBARA: My husband and I bought this piece of junk at the Galeries Lafayette and this piece of junk is the number one witness to my downfall I was more intelligent than him he'd open the dictionary and tell me a word and say what does that mean? They were complicated words I didn't know them and he'd say: see how stupid you are ... *(A noise interrupts her. Light on JACQUELINE's horn.)*

JACQUELINE: Hello again! I've never been separated from this washbasin I coughed up my lungs in it and my life changed why did I cough in it instead of someplace else in the toilet or in the sink because it's my favorite basin I wash my vegetables in it a whole basin full of blood in the middle of the night in January 1957 overnight nothing was ever the same I told the doctor I've got TB he said: of course not it could be your stomach there are antibiotics for that I wasn't afraid I became contagious overnight I had to go away you shouldn't isolate people with tuberculosis you shouldn't isolate them it's stupid to isolate them I read a paper on the treatment of tuberculosis in the Soviet Union they're more intelligent there you can't go out as long as you've got the germs three months without seeing my children and sick people everywhere those huge iron gates the doctor said: you don't often see such beautiful germs such a splendid hole in your lungs you don't catch tuberculosis why hide behind that illness instead of another. *(A noise interrupts her. Light on* ANGÈLE'S *horn.)*

ANGÈLE: With Marcel and me it was love at first sight our signal was when I'd put this dress on in the morning with my smock over it Marcel would check out my dress and he'd know it was okay for that evening Marcel the bike and the rest and I'd take off my smock and lift up my dress and hop on the bike he had a big motorcycle we'd go off and do what we had to do he did it really well and we liked doing it as long as possible not like with Abel Marcel wasn't handsome but he had beautiful hands an artist's hands he worked in a factory he'd grab my cheek between his thumb and index finger and pull it from left to right several times a day I'd look in his eyes and I understood what he wanted to say all those things you can never say with words and I'd blush I enjoyed sex with Marcel I couldn't believe that you could enjoy yourself so much with that thing considering that that thing has such a bad reputation. ... *(A noise interrupts her. Light on* JACQUELINE'S *horn.)*

JACQUELINE: Hello again! So after the operation I was at the teachers' convalescent home in Maisons-Lafitte the teachers' insurance company place I felt validated there I said to myself: Jacqueline is learning a trade I was living with my Russian at the time but I wasn't pulling my weight he was a painter he put a lot of faith in what I said about his painting he'd say: tell me what's not right and if I said: there's something there that's not right he'd take a look and he'd change everything but I didn't know anything about painting and he was a big reader he read a lot I had been trained as a short-hand typist! Thank you ... *(A noise interrupts her. Light on* BARBARA'S *horn.)*

BARBARA: When we met he was a cook in Lille and I was a receptionist at the same hotel he was six years younger than me he wanted to go out with me I was put off by the age difference so I said: yeah sure enough of that. ... *(A noise interrupts her. Light on* BARBARA'S *horn.)* He'd serve the staff but not me he'd call me "bitch" he'd say: tonight she'll eat shit he was angry he was vulgar once a customer forgot his shoes and he returned them as a favor to me so I offered him a drink! That customer's shoes started everything between us 12 years of hell 12 shitty years I spent being bored to tears. … *(A noise interrupts her. Light on* BARBARA*'s horn.)* He was always throwing pots and pans around he had a nasty character and even though he had talent at the stove the boss threw him out that was before the shoes he came to live with us at our café in the North he'd sleep in my room I slept with Maman Papa slept alone he lost a leg in the First World War there was the café with a kitchen next to it through a door! A little wooden staircase a large hallway with our three bedrooms the room at the end for Mom the middle one for my sister and the first room was a hole in the wall … *(A noise interrupts her. Light on* ANGÈLE*'s horn.)*

ANGÈLE: Marcel would pinch my cheeks and I was so happy! To do what we had to do he'd have to take off my dress … *(A noise interrupts her. Light on* BARBARA*'s horn.)*

BARBARA: There was another spiral staircase that went up to the first floor and over the café and the kitchen there was a big dance hall for banquets and then over our bedroom there was a big room and a little bedroom with this painting in it! *(*EVE *brings over a painting wrapped in brown paper.)* Papa stole it from the Germans he really liked it one day my father died we heard him yell he was covered with blood it was coming out of his mouth and he fell his arms folded across his body it was an aneurism it was Pentecost Monday I came down with jaundice I didn't cry but I came down with jaundice my cook cleaned everything up he washed him and prepared the body so I held onto him did I hold on too much? Was it too soon? Was it a mistake? He cheated on me with the switchboard operator we got married right away … *(A noise interrupts her. Light on* JACQUELINE*'s horn.)*

JACQUELINE: Hello again! after that we lived in the 16th in a maid's room at a Dutchwoman's home she had a large apartment near Kleber when we went into our room the skylight fell into the gutter I had just had my third baby the Dutchwoman was adorable she was a wreck divorced an alcoholic her husband had a cushy job her children looked down on her I found her one day on the servants' stairs covered with blood she'd fallen she was a big-hearted woman she lent me the key to her kitchen. … *(A noise interrupts her. Light on* ANGÈLE*'s horn.)*

ANGÈLE: And when I was completely naked in front of Marcel I'd think about Abel about Maman and Papa and the Holy Virgin but she must really understand these things since it was about love Marcel was married too and I'd say to him: what we're doing is bad and he'd say: I want to kiss you Angèle he was crazy about this dress because you can see my body that's what Marcel would say: that dress moves with your body "that dress moves with your body." Marcel really had a way with words and he was stubborn too so he got me thanks to the Electricity Company … *(A noise interrupts her. Light on* JACQUELINE*'s horn.)*

JACQUELINE: The Dutchwoman … Hello again …was evicted the police commissioner told her: we're going to seal up the place and to me he said you're in the room upstairs? Alright so go back up there and he shut off the meter and the electric stove after that we met a Dominican son of a wholesale champagne salesman who liked artists he knew some worker priests who lived in the 13th district near the Chevaleret subway stop behind the Say sugar refineries they had an old house so we moved to the 13th I still had my washbasin the famous washbasin where I'd coughed up my lungs we'd put everything in it nails thumbtacks fuses screws paper clips rubber bike tire patches fertilizer clothes pins rubber bands a hand saw and even a crucifix it's a large washbasin as you can see … *(A noise interrupts her.* EVE *sets off a different, continuous sound and sets up three stools next to each other. Then she interrupts that sound.)*

IGOR *(Into a microphone)*: Ladies, come over and sit down! *(They come over and sit down.)*

EVE: Who wants to begin?

ANGÈLE : I do!

Eve: Angèle Rougeot!

Angèle: I used to be a welder I admired female singers and when Zappy Max came along with his "boom boom tralala" radio game show one of my sisters said: okay Lucienne Delyle Zappy's waiting for you I adored Lucienne Delyle after meals they'd say: sing us a song I'd imitate Lucienne Delyle and everybody'd say: Oh you sound just like Lucienne Delyle I made myself a fitted dress with green stripes and blue polka dots but Zappy didn't want me! *(She sings "The Lovers of Saint-Jean.")* And at my sister's wedding June 5 1937 another 5th of June everybody said: sing a song for us so I imitated Lucienne Delyle and everybody said: oh it's just like Lucienne Delyle my sister's wedding left a mark on my life we made a splash at the town hall I was wearing a long blue taffetas dress and gloves my parents had rented a bus Robert my brother-in-law was smoking Naja cigarettes and I admired him because of the Najas I prefer yellow to dark tobacco June 5th was Saint Angèle's day and my brother-in-law broke off a carnation from my sister's bouquet and came over to me and said: happy Saint's day my little chickadee at my wedding all I had to wear was a suit so I told myself: I'll just wear a suit and nothing on my head since that's the way it is! I didn't imitate Lucienne Delyle Mother would read all my letters she read the one in which Abel said do you remember our little room on the Rue des Pyrénées Mother said: you get married right away before you have a child "you little . . ." I said: why do you read my letters you've no right and she said: this letter is worse than if you slapped me so I slapped her and she slapped me back! Mother was a real disciplinarian she was a protestant all this because during the war Abel was very thin and he was standing on the platform at the Nation subway stop and so was I I was eating those vitamin enriched cakes they gave us during the war and Abel said to me: aren't there any for me? I gave him two I was a good-hearted person then the subway came he followed me into the subway I said to myself: this soldier must have really suffered and the next thing I knew I was married to him all because of a cake the day I married Abel I knew I didn't love him he was lazy he was from an Italian background Mother kept asking: Abel's not a French name what is it? What the hell did it matter to her if it was French or not he had a long nail on his little finger he played the guitar you know what I mean I hated my Mother.

Eve *(Interrupting Angèle)*: Who wants to continue?

Barbara *(Jumping right in)*: He wanted a daughter a blond with blue eyes but he had varicoceles his sperm was no good varicoceles that's varicose veins on the testicles he got them from the heat of the ovens those veins drove him crazy as if he weren't already crazy enough he was completely covered with them he was a Cordon Bleu chef and he found work in a canteen that wasn't good enough for the gentleman between the canteen and his varicoceles he lost it we left the North and came to Paris to the Prince de Galles hotel he had connections I was a dishwasher and he was a cook he cheated on me with the switchboard operator another switchboard operator we'd get into fights and throw just about everything at each other: Swiss cheese scissors a plant the cork screw he drank a lot once it was a crystal decanter a gift from my sister well anyway considering what my sister did to me later in 42 Mother was 42-years-old and pregnant with me but she didn't know it she'd tell herself: oh it's menopause already but something was moving in her stomach that was me moving and they pulled me out with forceps that effected my brain I had some minor psychomotor problems I didn't like milk and my sister who's twenty years older than me forced me to drink it I'd throw everything up and she'd start all over with the bowl of milk and I'd throw up on her she'd beat me and she was a teacher a real pedagogue! My sister traumatized me Papa would beat my mother who'd beat my sister who'd beat me my grandmother would beat my grandfather as for my great grandmother Victoire everybody beat her so slaps in the face I know about those and papa had fought in World War I and World War II he fought so much against the Germans that he didn't talk anymore my mother would beat Sultane she'd tie her up I'd untie her and my mother'd tie me up for over an hour in Sultane's kennel so then papa would beat me too after Sultane we had Boby who died it was my fault my mother was working in her café in the North papa was at his brother's in a tannery in Touraine so Boby would take me to school and one day I walked in front of Boby he was behind me it was 20 minutes after one a truck came along and ran over Boby I should have waited for him after that I had Carole I'd brush her really well but then I left for boarding school so she died I'm a bilingual switchboard operator at the Normandy-Holiday Inn but I don't want anybody to kiss me they all want to kiss me! I like being an operator I listen to people I bought a new car I live alone with my dog Hélène when Hélène dies I'll buy a cat ...

Eve: Jacqueline!

Jacqueline *(Jumping right in)*: The Rue des Ecoles is the street of love for me passionate love I was 17 my Russian guy had a big mouth you'd think he was whistling we'd say: that guy's a nice guy because he whistles no his mouth was just made that way that his paintings were tormented all dark with Prussian blues big paintings horrible things that had to come out people didn't like them I was a country girl with a certain naïveté about me he'd say I was his Greek statue my daughters had a really hard time with the Brigitte Bardot fashion you had to lose tons of weight! He was 24 seven years older than me he made a big impression on me he was awfully thin it wasn't his nature to be fat but this man who had suffered so was impressive I enjoyed the sex right away I was new at it what a surprise they needed high school students at the Reuilly barracks to volunteer to welcome the prisoners back from Germany the trains would arrive at the Gare de l'Est station they were deloused and given numbers there were police check ups it was exhilarating the war was over we'd sing "Sambre et Meuse" but there wasn't any more jam we young folks did our bit with him it was love at first sight he had a room in the barracks next to the office where he worked during the day as an interpreter I was fascinated by his eyes his burning eyes and his mouth my mother said that since I was making love in a barracks I was a slut after that we moved to the Rue des Ecoles but there was a problem he was married to a woman who'd had a child with a German that created problems with the paperwork so he sacrificed himself but then he also got her pregnant he must have loved her I read all their letters and then I burned them that's when my mother ruined everything she sent the cops after me: missing persons and all that and since I was already a sinner I had made my communion I broke all contact with my mother I moved in with an aunt one of my father's sisters who was no longer speaking to my mother I met her at my father's funeral I said I lived with her I found a job S.O.S. Shut up Obey and Serve S.O.S and then at an insurance company! After that it was the Bohemian life he painted a lot of Christ faces he was born in Lithuania that was the truth he said he'd been to China that wasn't the truth he was a born liar we'd eat oatmeal cooked in cod liver oil I was J3 meaning I got the most ration cards for milk and sugar I'd sell my sugar and buy pearl barley and bird seed at the bird market and we'd eat the seeds he'd paint the kitchens of old broads and hung wallpaper that's how I found out that my little broom wasn't a broom after all I'd say to him: don't lose my broom and he'd say it's not a broom I had it a really long time and now I can't find it I kept it for 26 years it could reach under the furniture and in the corners it was really well made now I don't have anything because of all the moves people say three moves add up to a fire ... *(Eve offers Jacqueline a wallpaper hanger's brush.)* My broom! ... it wasn't a broom after all I learned that much later on it's called a wallpaper hanger's brush I always called it a little broom I took it with me everywhere to the camp grounds it would sweep inside and outside an ideal little broom you know it's all about the bristles very stiff bristles my camping tent is very important the first one was pyramid not Canadian style there's an ad that says no cramps when you camp well we crawled in a cramped two by two meter tent that's a pure camping tradition sometimes we'd sleep outside and when there'd be a drizzle at one o'clock in the morning we'd run back into the tent we were at home after that we got a big ordinary Lafuma tent with an awning I had seven children with my Russian guy on the Rue des Ecoles by the way there's a store called "The Old Camper's Place" it's for camping ...

Eve: Are you finished?

Barbara: No. ... Listen! *(Now it's her turn to jump in. She gets up and comes to the front of the stage.)* I was 33 years old the doorbell rang I was living on Poulet Street it was the Prince de Galles switchboard operator a redhead her lips were pinched she was haggard looking she was living on the Avenue d'Italie she was unrecognizable! One day my husband said: can you go over to the Avenue d'Italie for me? Near where his floosie lived but he didn't know that I knew where she lived anyway he had lots of floosies everywhere at Nation in Vincennes in the 14th district once I caught him with a floosie in Neuilly he said that she was a business colleague at work yeah sure doing business in the sack! He was working in insurance at the time he had gone on throwing his pans around so he'd got out of there and gone into insurance so I went to the Avenue d'Italie with my dog Hélène and Hélène ran into a building it seemed familiar to her she goes up to the second floor and calls my husband not a word he doesn't budge I knocked on the door I said I knew he was with his floosie but later he said: she's not my floosie! So the floosie, poor thing, she asks me where my husband is: Where's Lionel? Four of her teeth were missing but she had it where it counts she was quite something but that's got nothing to do with it the redhead was a wreck I offered her some martini she was sobbing and I said: drink up Monique you'll feel better her name was Monique and she kept on Lionel here and Lionel there and I kept on with: drink up Monique and she was drinking up my martini I got it all out of her and then I put her to bed she was drunk on Martini when my husband got home I said: your operator is in my bed I took my coat my gloves and my dog and I went out for a walk for an hour after that she was crying on the stairs he'd hit her she had blood on her suit! With my husband it was about passion I had a nervous breakdown because of my husband my body wasn't retaining calcium I wasn't retaining magnesium I wasn't retaining anything at all I fainted on the stairs the doctor gave me a shot of Valium I stayed in bed my cornea became infected I was completely handicapped I took care of handicapped people in Evian during the Algerian War Evian during the Algerian war was something else Papa would take me there in his Citroen it had been searched because of the Evian meetings there were bombs the casino blew up and the mayor was killed there were handsome riot policemen I was nineteen I had a really great time in Evian Fats Domino was there I always liked Sidney Bechet I cried at his funeral the casino was repaired and we danced at the casino then I left for England and I learned English things weren't ordinary at that time

I fell in love for the first time not with an Englishman a Spaniard who was also learning English after that I was a hostess at the Lille airport that time of the Algerian war is a wonderful memory.

IGOR *(Voiceover on the microphone)*: Good evening, ladies! Barbara come over here closer closer … *(BARBARA has come over to stage front.)* According to you, why do you think you were chosen?

BARBARA: Because I'm interesting you told me I was interesting!

IGOR: And you Jacqueline?

JACQUELINE: Thank you for choosing me. … Thank you … During the Algerian War my mother died and so did one of my brothers he was there they died at the same time she in Auvergne she had left Paris he in Algeria he had written that Arabs were being buried alive he had had scurvy I bought black stockings a black coat black gloves I took the train for Auvergne I stopped on the way I couldn't go on I said to myself: what's the use it's useless I was thinking of my dead brother all alone in Algeria I didn't cry for my mother because of my brother I cried for my brother after that there was the important miners' strike in '63 I was working at the Bagnolet town hall and the town hall organized a solidarity action I bought a rain coat and left for the North I met the elected officials and all the unions of the town of Escaudain it was Easter vacation I brought back 50 children to Bagnolet I wasn't familiar with the North it's nice there I thought of my mother I had responsibilities she dreamt that I would become a school teacher in the train with the miners' children I cried for my mother I went to the bathroom and cried for her after that things were definitely over with my Russian I was relieved! …

IGOR: And you Angèle Rougeot?

ANGÈLE: When the Germans arrived in Paris Mother said we're going to Bordeaux to your sister's house there were four of us sisters I said: I'm staying in Paris and she said: so the Germans can rape you, "You little …" she said that a lot "You little ..." we left for Bordeaux we found ourselves in the city of Sens we camped out in railroad cars my father worked in the Paris public transportation system we had connections so we were given a postal car with a bathroom there were a lot of soldiers I was 14 I did my best to look 17 and I did look 17 I had made myself a little green and yellow dress with balloon sleeves and a red collar it was horrible the cows were screaming they needed to be milked people were fleeing rabbits and pigs were being killed on the farms Mother had lost six kilos she was very worried about Papa after that we left but we made another mistake and ended up in the village of Chalus near Limoges and it was just as horrible there the cows were screaming the rabbits and pigs too Mother was going crazy the planes were dropping bombs everywhere and we were underneath them we were yelling we were afraid a soldier grabbed me by the waist and we dove into the clover and the bombs stopped then he started to sing just like that all of a sudden he started to sing because he had been afraid because I was afraid because it was war I was wearing my dress with the balloon sleeves and the little red collar and he was singing in the clover and there were people yelling and dying and Mother called: Angèle Angèle and I was listening to the soldier singing it's a really good memory that place Chalus near Limoges after that we went back to Paris we found Papa there we all started crying he had lost weight too we couldn't stop crying especially me it did me good to cry Mother and Papa and my sisters too so we cried for three days it was so good and then Papa turned on the radio and what did I hear the soldier from Chalus singing and the announcer saying: that was Georges Guétary so I called one of my sisters and said: that guy in the clover was Georges and she said: write to him to your Georges I wrote him at his radio station and he answered with a photograph saying the soldier wasn't him but he would have liked to have known the girl with the red collar in the clover in fact that soldier was imitating Georges Guétary so I was chosen because I am sincere!

IGOR: Thank you, ladies! Eve!

EVE *(Singing while she's handing out three little presents that she shows the audience before giving them to each contestant, calling out their names each time. When she's finished she says into the microphone:)* Jacqueline!

Jacqueline *(Stage front)*: I was without a man for years but I wanted one I'd look at their butts and backs in the subway and then our union introduced me to two men from Portugal who were having problems with their boss I had to meet with the work inspector to help them one was older than the other the older one had five children in Portugal he was anti-his government he wanted a revolution we got together I was growing parsley and thyme in my washbasin in Bagnolet because he liked thyme he was a mason you don't mess with my children it wasn't easy for him he was quite the family man he was unhappy he'd say he was living with children who didn't love him he wasn't seeing the ones he loved and when he did he wouldn't recognize them he wanted a child here in France I had closed down shop for over ten years but I started up again and number eight was extra special today women have children when they decide to: oh no I don't want to have one and then if I want to have one it's easy I took out my contraceptive and we waited six months and nothing then it was De Gaulle's funeral everybody had the day off we made love and it worked I went to the clinic where they'd introduced the painless birth method I was feeling great I was polishing furniture they teach you to listen to the child growing inside of you I'd like to be a surrogate mother and make children every year for women who want them if you're interested Ladies let me know the Portuguese guy was confused because I enjoyed making love and that big strong macho guy didn't understand in Portugal it's the whorehouse first then a frigid wife because of religion so the word whore was frequently used all because I was the one calling the shots I discovered France with him Deauville the Côte d'Azur we went swimming in November in Bandol Belgium Switzerland we had a taste for life in general and then he had his mid-life crisis he told me women were coming on to him in the subway and then I discovered the worst he was having an affair he said: I don't want my son to find another guy in my bed and I said: that's tough my ass belongs to me and one night I almost killed him with a knife finally we made a deal he'd take the kid to the Trône fair on Sundays but then came the July revolution the military coup d'état in Portugal in '74 the Fascist government was overthrown he was expecting that but he'd waited so long he'd stopped waiting and then he found himself another cash cow a woman like me with children so one day I said: you were in such a hurry to make your revolution to find a hundred others like yourself ready to take up a rifle well they took up the rifles over there and you're here how come? now he lives in Portugal I got married at 50 to see what it was like he was a young man who'd broken with his family he wanted to play a joke on them we gave them a run for their money but we didn't get along he left for Portugal but he's not Portuguese he worked in an office he bought us furniture a dining room set and silverware I got rid of everything the dining room set and the silver a plate a bowl my toothbrush a comb soap I'm happy I asked the cultural services to get me tickets for the Japanese wrestling match I like sports: basketball volley ball racing shot putt high jumping canoeing horse racing and most of all mountain climbing. Okay Thank you. *(Pointing to her photograph: she's shown mountain climbing.)* That's me! *(She goes out to the wings.)*

Eve *(Into the microphone)*: Angèle!

Angèle *(Stage front)*: I'm convinced I killed my Mother she had health problems she wasn't all there mentally so one Sunday I went to see her and I stupidly said to her: we really blew it dear mother we didn't know how to love each other and she started to cry her chin was shaking her nose was running and I just went on I couldn't stop I told her she had ruined our lives my sister's and mine and hers as well and especially papa's he was a good natured fellow but he'd changed because of her she kept on crying instead of stopping I went on telling myself a few tears will do her good and papa will be happier afterwards the next day papa said your mother had a bad night come quickly so I went and she looked at me with such harsh eyes she said: I had to pee all night long Angèle it's the emotion you shouldn't have upset me and I said: un huh! an "un huh" like that very cold and I could see she was surprised but I didn't say anything just that "un huh" we looked at each other like that for a moment and I went to work at work there was a voice inside me that kept saying: go quickly and kiss her one last time she's going to die because of you so after work I ran and went into her room she was asleep I didn't dare kiss her I was afraid it would wake her up her face was calm and soft and I went home Papa came to get me in the middle of the night he was yelling it's mother it's mother that's all he could say so I started to cry I had already understood and he kept on yelling: it's mother it's mother so we ran to her room she was in the same position as the night before her face was calm and soft I even noticed that she had beautiful eyebrows I told Papa to stop yelling and call the doctor the doctor said she was in a coma it had probably been a cerebral hemorrhage she'd have to have brain surgery she'd taken too many tranquilizers and her organs were shutting down so we waited I'd call Necker hospital every day and they'd tell me: no change we stayed with Papa and made him meals he drank a lot at dinner that would make him want to laugh so we'd say: go ahead laugh Papa laugh Mother's going to come out of it but I knew I had killed her with my "un huh" so harsh and so cold at the end of the week when they told us she had died that her brain wasn't functioning anymore I made myself a very simple black dress we went to pick up the ashes at the morgue and when I saw her name written on the box of ashes I burst into tears I opened the box and I said: it's not possible it's not possible those warm ashes aren't mother Robert had smoked so many Najas that they killed him we watched him go downhill we went to the hospital every day and we'd say: Robert how are you? you had to say something and he'd look at us with those eyes his eyes were really something it was horrible to see he had blue eyes they're harder to bare than brown eyes he didn't say anything he just looked at us he was unrecognizable after that his disease went to his head and he went crazy at the funeral I wore the dress I made for mother's funeral the simple black one they lived with my sister in Saint-Mandé-Tourelle they had had premature twins they would walk them on Sundays in the Vincennes woods I don't like the Vincennes woods anymore Saint Mandé-Tourelle either it's like the Saint-Ambroise subway! Another subway! I was working with one of my sisters in Saint-Ambroise in a plastics factory and one day when I was coming out of the subway she burst into tears and said: Paul died another one and I said: it's not true tell me it's not true he was 56 years old and she said: yes it was his heart when I get out at Saint-Ambroise I see Paul's eyes his beautiful blue eyes he had blue eyes too Marcel says: so why get off at the Saint-Ambroise stop! Last year the doctor told us: you have to put Marcel in the hospital another one he had trouble swallowing just as a joke Marcel asked the doctor if he was going to kick the bucket the doctor told him it was a tumor when I heard the word tumor I couldn't feel my legs anymore Abel had already died of a tumor we weren't going to start all over again with Marcel when he was hospitalized I lost two kilos but Marcel kept his good humor he'd say to me: you remember the 1954 dress Angèle when I'd take it off you'd say: be careful Marcel the material is fragile he wanted to reassure me he'd say: I never knew if I preferred you with it on or off it's a beautiful dress but you weren't so bad yourself and I was thinking tumor tumor another tumor they took his out it was in the salivary glands Marcel handled the operation well he was from Normandy I said: you're really something Marcel and three days later he was dead it was winter I bought a black coat and hat my father had given me his chimes and I gave them to my son who is the love of my life I still have Robert's carnation I pray to God for the souls of all those who have died my life is very simple I live on Picpus street and I love you all! ... Thank you so much! *(She goes out into the wings.)*

Eve *(Into the microphone)*: Barbara!

Barbara *(Stage front)*: One day I lost my face it became square before it was elongated from tightening my jaw and all the muscles around it I lost it overnight it was a different face so I focused on my extremities: my nails my shoes my hair my husband said I looked like a cashier in a department store he was right I had that look the look of a department store cashier I wanted a divorce he wouldn't come home for weeks when I said: I want a divorce he started to cry we went to bed and after that to the Galeries Lafayette and a ray of sunlight fell on my calves on the boulevard Haussmann all of a sudden I felt happy I was a beautiful woman and I liked my legs so I started walking fast on those legs I told myself: enjoy your legs while you still have them and he tried to follow me I was walking fast on purpose he had started to gain weight we went into the Galeries Lafayette and we bought this piece of junk in thirty seconds because of a ray of sunlight but also because he saw that I was beautiful on the boulevard Haussmann the salesman told us: it makes a beautiful half yellow half pink light actually it's mostly pink and when we got out of the Galeries Lafayette the sun was gone and

I said to myself: no more sun that's a bad sign I was afraid I looked at my Lionel who was looking at a young woman with a beautiful derriere and that's when I said to myself: you too you'll be cheated on ten days later he was cheated on by a Belgian from Spa the day of the lamp I was wearing a beret we went home and I kept my beret on why not? It was Saint Valentine's Day my name is Barbara but my other name is Valentine Lionel knew very well that my other name was Valentine so I said to him: Lionel it's Saint Valentine's day and he said: I have a toothache and went to the bathroom to take some vitamin enriched aspirin and from the bathroom he asks me what's for "chow" he said "chow" and I couldn't stand that so I said: duck with grapefruit and he says: oh good it's Chinese! He said "it's Chinese" with a contemptuous tone in his voice as if he were saying what a jerk you are you poor thing it was like he'd stuck a knife in me I couldn't stand that either I still wasn't retaining any potassium everything went dark and I turned on this piece of junk and its light was half yellow half pink like the salesman said mostly pink the day's pleasure was spoiled I started to sob I took off my beret with one sharp gesture and I too went into the bathroom to comb my hair he was coming out I said: why shouldn't I keep my beret on during dinner that's acceptable he said: we're not in a restaurant and then he added: you think you're in an old movie I once played an extra in *The Longest Day* I didn't even recognize myself in that film there were scallops but I didn't have much of an appetite it was Saint Valentine's Day so I said: you've been cheated on with a Belgian guy he threw *TV Guide* at me he wanted to strangle me I got away and he caught his foot in this piece of junk and he fell and so did the piece of junk it lit up the carpet I didn't digest the scallops well I cried at our divorce hearing and he cried too sex isn't enough between a couple I kept this piece of junk because of that half-yellow half pink light mostly pink!

Eve *(Into the microphone)*: Thank you, Barbara.

Barbara: I'm not finished ... Everything I love is in my sideboard my cake tin in the shape of a fish the fish represents Christ it's a rare object my cabbage-shaped terrine in trompe-l'oeil my 19th-century soup tureen with its trompe-l'oeil handles another trompe-l'oeil my Breton spoon holder my porcelain mustard jar with little rabbits my little 1925 egg cups my Baccarat punch bowl my really solid silver candlestick my gold-edged Limoges china assorted dessert plates dishes that go with the sauce boats that go with my Couson cutlery box my Le Creuset Dutch oven my little animal salt and pepper shakers: the owl the pig the frog! The painting stolen from the Germans represents Nefertiti! *(She shows us the "little animal" pepper shaker: the owl.)*

JACQUELINE and ANGÈLE join BARBARA stage front. JACQUELINE shows them a magazine on which you can see the reproduction of a painting.

JACQUELINE: That's me, completely naked, at 17.

ANGÈLE's dress lights up. EVE offers a piece of cake to the three contestants, singing "C'est magnifique." Many little photographs [stage left] light up one after the other. The four women eat their pieces of cake as they look out at the audience ... IGOR thanked them—maybe?

Translation made possible by the generous support of Etant donnés, the French-American Fund for the Performing Arts, a program of FACE.

Cut

Emmanuelle Marie

Translated by Michael Taormina

AUTHOR'S NOTE

Because the author was present during the production of the play, it goes without saying that the form of the text very well may have changed over the course of rehearsals, right up until the public premiere.

The stage directions have been added only for the sake of ease and reading comprehension; I leave the choice of space and décor to the imagination of the director.

Similarly, I leave to the director the choice of the number of actors on stage. The Chorus of Women may indeed comprise from two to *n* actors. However, it should be noted that this text requires at least three actors.

The order of scenes is not gratuitous, and I respectfully ask that it be observed.

I believe that these aspects of the text will invite a genuine collaboration between author and director.

I ask future readers to keep these things in mind and thank you in advance.

CUT (k t) vt (cut) couper, trancher;—one's nails, se couper les ongles / couper (slash);—one's finger, se couper le doigt / couper, croiser (cross) / couper, réduire, abréger (shorten) / tailler (diamond) / couper (a coat) / couper (cards) / ART CULINAIRE. Découper / CINÉMA. faire le montage de (a film) / ARTS graver / AUTOMOBILES—a corner close, prendre un tournant à la corde / FINANCES réduire (wages).

LAROUSSE English-French

*In the basement of a bar, restaurant, or hotel, three flights below street level. A spacious women's bathroom, with closed doors in the rear, tiles, neon-lights, sinks, and mirrors, perhaps. A woman (*Woman 1*), alone, seated next to a table bearing a small sign that reads: "$1 gratuity requested. Thank you."*

Woman 1: Don't expect men to sit down when they pee.

Men don't sit down. They pee standing up, against the wall. Some men will do anything to spy on women, like peek through a keyhole, just to watch them pee. I've seen it. But not here. Not in my ladies' room.

The women in my ladies' room sit down when they pee. That is how they pee. And that is how I want them to pee.

Of course, women sometimes squat when they have to pee in the middle of nowhere. Nature calls, and you squat.

In any event, they could pee standing up, like a man, if they wanted.

My grandmother, who was a sailor, used to wear crotchless panties so she could pee standing up. She would stand there, with her feet firmly planted on deck, next to a drain, and that's how she would relieve herself. The liquid never ran down her legs and it was done with the utmost discretion, beneath her petticoats.

But your city-women, your urban gals, your civilized ladies, they all pee sitting down.

When they have to go, they pull their pants and underwear down to the knee, or they pull their skirts up to avoid soiling the fabric and they let loose. The zipper unzips, the undergarments rustle, the silk slithers, the khaki breathes, as they open themselves to the world … And the music, I hear the music of women taking a piss …

Just then a door opens; WOMAN 2 enters. As she speaks to WOMAN 1, she attends to her appearance before a mirror, imaginary or not: washing her hands, straightening her stockings on her calf, readjusting that silk slip which tends to twist out of place on women with a slim waist and hips ... blablabla, etc. ... and she does it all with perfect grace and charm and ... blahblahblah, etc.

WOMAN 2: I do sometimes take a moment for myself, I admit, to daydream just a little, while I wait for it to be over. Perhaps the seated position which a woman assumes during urination induces a meditative state, it lasts a few seconds. A stillness descends. Body relaxed, spine straight, the world half asleep, as she contemplates the door of the stall, the supreme nothing, a kind of grace unique to the urinal.

Just then, a door opens and WOMAN 3 enters.

WOMAN 3: And what if she held back ...

WOMAN 2: Legs closed, muscles flexed, teeth clenched, bladder throbbing.

WOMAN 3: When she finally manages to forget herself, it's like she's in heaven.

WOMAN 2: The tension leaves her body, and her mind is clear.

WOMAN 3: Like Buddha, smiling.

WOMAN 2: A kind of grace, I'm telling you, it's a kind of grace. Suspended over the toilet.

WOMAN 3: I say: heaven. An angelic, incorporeal feeling.

WOMAN 1: And yet it's piss. *(A pause.)*

WOMAN 2: And only silence, silence, a peaceful ecstasy to piss in.

Woman 3: Nothing will ever stop us from sitting down to piss.

Woman 2: Nothing, ever. It's our trademark. The trademark of our sex. Praise be to God!

Woman 3: Indeed.

Woman 1: As the nymphs aim their warm jets of piss in the bowl, I listen to the music, I hear the music they make: the only sound is that of water. Water. Water music. Sometimes it makes a tinny sound like water hitting stainless steel. Sometimes it is a whisper, growing louder, till it suddenly stops. Or it is soft and delicate, almost apologetic, so sorry for pissing, we're oh so sorry for pissing, for pissing how we piss.

Woman 3 *(Speaking in confidence)*: As a matter of fact, I must admit that I try to avoid pissing in public urinals … for all sorts of reasons. Mostly on account of the noise the urine makes as it falls in the ivory bowl. It's embarrassing, what a noise for strange ears.

Woman 1: There is no reason to be ashamed of a good piss. That's how the Good Lord made us, we're all pissers. All God's creatures piss. And piss makes noise. I can recognize a woman just by the noise she makes.

I say to myself: ah, *that's* the music of the girl who works behind the bar, a real go-getter, she's always in a hurry it's so busy. Ah, *that's* the owner. I'd recognize her music anywhere. She takes her time now, her getting older and all. She relishes these moments of calm and solitude. Besides, she is the boss.

Some women have no faith. No faith: I can tell by the noise *that one* is making that she has used almost the whole roll of toilet paper to decorate the seat before she sits down.

Woman 3 *(To Woman 1)*: I like to make sure there is plenty of paper to unroll. I fold it piece by piece, then spread it carefully around the toilet seat, keeping watch that no strange drop of urine has soiled it.

Woman 1 *(To Woman 3)*: I have enormous respect for women, that's why

my toilet bowls sparkle. I myself inspect each toilet after each use.
(To the public.) Every hour of every day, every minute, every second—there it is—I am reminded. With every flush, on the face of every woman, I am reminded. This is the face of nature, and thousands of voices cry out:
"Remember! You are part of creation. Nothing more, nothing less! And the same goes for all your kind. You are only human. Nothing more, nothing less! Part of creation!" But women are deeply modest, they recognize this.

WOMAN 2: Women are deeply modest.

WOMAN 3: Women are deeply modest.

WOMAN 1: The only toilets I clean are women's. Men don't come here.

WOMAN 2: They don't?

WOMAN 3: No, they don't.

WOMAN 1: They wait outside the door. They never come in. I mean never.

WOMAN 2: Never?

WOMAN 3: You heard the lady: never!

WOMAN 1: Never, not even when the men's bathroom is crowded. But the men's bathroom is rarely crowded anyway. In my bathroom, that's a different story. Women often have to wait.

WOMAN 2: We are often obliged to wait.

WOMAN 3: We often wait.

WOMAN 1: They wait because the female urethra is so narrow, and their sphincter not very powerful. The ladies spend plenty of time in my bathroom. And that is why my cup jingles with money. And ladies tip more than gentlemen.

Chorus of Women 2 and 3 *(Whispering)*: That is why her cup jingles with money.

Woman 1: It's my secret joy.

Chorus of Women 2 and 3: It's her secret joy.

Woman 1: This is my secret joy: when there is music and my cup jingles with money.

Chorus of Women 2 and 3: This is her secret joy: when there is music …

Woman 1: And my cup jingles with money. *(Silence.)*
God's creation provides for me. The Good Lord made his creatures pissers for my secret joy. Because no one escapes a pressing need, a natural urge, a trip to the outhouse. Because no one escapes her own nature. Nature always has the upper hand. Nature always gets the best of you, for better or for worse. I have enormous respect for nature, which made you the way you are, with your narrow urethra …

Woman 2: A narrow urethra …

Woman 3: And a not so powerful sphincter.

Woman 2: Not very powerful …

Woman 3: I was just thinking that dogs don't make such a fuss.

Woman 2: Dogs?

Woman 1: There is no shame in being one of God's creatures, madam.
A woman, a man, a dog, we're all the same

WOMAN 3: Do you think that God is a dog?

WOMAN 1: A dog?

WOMAN 3: A dog ...

WOMAN 1: God is God, madam.

WOMAN 3: Do you think God is a woman?

WOMAN 1: I believe God has no sex, Madam.

WOMAN 3: He is no doubt sexless. That's why you always see God represented with a full beard. And we know that the only other people who wear beards are dogs and women.

WOMAN 2: We know that!?

WOMAN 3: Tell me, madam, are you so proud to think you know the sex of God? *(Silence.)* My mother cried her eyes out the day I was born. She cried so much, the doctor scolded her. "What is all this crying?" he asked. "I wanted a boy," she said," but it's a girl." *(Silence.)* If only God had been a woman.

Surely my mother, who was so devout, would have cried less when I was born. *(Silence. The three women are quiet, fixing themselves before the mirror.)*

My mother always used to say, she would say: "Close your legs, you little hussy. And keep them closed. Close your legs, bite your lip, and tuck in that butt. Do it, and be still." She always said the same thing, always the same. *(Silence.)*

Things get more complicated when you're a little girl and you try to see what we have down there ... Lost in all the folds. You have to be a gymnast. Or use a mirror. I was no gymnast ... And even then, you can't see all of it. A woman's secret seems to continue on the inside, of herself, on the inside of herself.

CHORUS OF WOMEN *(Whispering)*: Close your legs! Close your legs! They might see your panties! God might see your panties! Close your legs! Bite your lip! Tuck in your butt!

WOMAN 3: No one wants to talk. No one will speak. I was no gymnast. Only you, my mirror, my beautiful mirror.

CHORUS OF WOMEN 1 AND 2: Close your legs! Close your legs! And keep them closed, you little hussy! Close your legs! Bite your lip! Tuck in that butt! Do it, and be still!

WOMAN 3: I took hold of the mirror: my mirror, my beautiful mirror …

CHORUS OF WOMEN 1 AND 2: Close your legs! Close your legs! They might see your panties!

WOMAN 3: And I … looked. At my vagina in the mirror. Look at my vagina in the mirror.

CHORUS OF WOMEN 1 AND 2: God might see you panties! Close your legs! Bite your lip! Tuck in your butt! Now pray!

WOMAN 3: Yes, I will pray, I pray for my soul and the devil whose eye is looking back at me, a devious eye in the mirror, looking at me. Maybe God sees me? Sees what I'm doing. Looking. Oh …

CHORUS OF WOMEN 1 AND 2: Close your legs! Bite your lip! Tuck in your butt! Now pray!

WOMAN 3: I pray for my soul for daring to look at my vagina in the mirror. I am the devil. But that's OK, no one can see. No one will know. I will tell no one. And if I pray for my soul, everything will be OK.

CHORUS OF WOMEN 1 AND 2: Now pray!

WOMAN 3: Yes, yes, I pray for my soul. How beautiful God is, how luminous in the church window. And the Virgin Mary, so beautiful, and the angels and all the saints in heaven are beautiful too. And all the little girls dressed in white on their way to the altar. My tiara is crooked, and the sleeves of my dress are too short. How can I receive God, when a little while ago the devil in the mirror was winking at me?

CHORUS OF WOMEN 1 AND 2: Now pray!

WOMAN 3: Ah, how devious, my hands smell like the devil. My hands smell like my secret. I must wash my hands and my soul. Quick! Quick! A confessional or a sink!

CHORUS OF WOMEN 1 AND 2: Close your legs, close your legs, you little hussy, and keep them closed!
Close your legs, close your legs, close your legs, you little hussy, and keep them closed! *(Continuing.)*

A WOMAN: Today is my first communion!
Things get more complicated when you're a little girl and you try to see what we have down there. All you have are your fingers to tell you what is on the inside, on the inside of yourself.

CHORUS OF WOMEN 1 AND 2: Close your legs, close your legs, you little hussy, and keep them closed!
Close your legs, close your legs, close your legs, you little hussy, and keep them closed! *(Continuing.)*

WOMAN 3: Yes, Father, I have sinned. I looked at my vagina in the mirror on the day of my first communion. I know it was wrong. Father, forgive me, I have sinned. All I have done, yes, and all I have failed to do. I have sinned. On the day of my first communion. *(Silence.)*

CHORUS OF WOMEN 1 AND 2: Now be still!

WOMAN 3: All I have done, yes, and all I have failed to do. On the day of my first communion.

CHORUS OF WOMEN 1 AND 2: Slut!

WOMAN 3: All I have done, yes, and all I have failed to do. On the day of my first communion.

CHORUS OF WOMEN 1 AND 2: Witch!

WOMAN 3: All I have done, yes, and all I have failed to do. On the day of my first communion.

CHORUS OF WOMEN 1 AND 2: Witch! Slut!

WOMAN 3: All I have done, yes, and all I have failed to do. On the day of my first communion.

CHORUS OF WOMEN 1 AND 2: Witch! Slut! Witch! Slut! Witch! Slut! Witch! *(Silence.)*

WOMAN 3: Shut up, little girl, be still: Or you will be burned alive. In the old days, others burned for much less …

WOMAN 2 *(Whispering)*: *Tais-toi ô ma fille tais-toi: Au bûcher autrefois, il y en a qui furent brûlées pour moins que ça …*
Tais-toi ô ma fille tais-toi: Au bûcher autrefois, il y en a qui furent brûlées pour moins que ça … (Silence.)

WOMAN 2: Imagine you're in French class.

CHORUS OF WOMEN 1 AND 3: *Que voyez-vous dans le tableau numéro 1? Dans le tableau numéro 1, je vois une fille.*

WOMAN 2: The professor is enunciating her vowels with extreme care. The mouth must be rounded and open to pronounce "o" and stretched tight as a smile to pronounce "é" the way the French do it.

CHORUS OF WOMEN 1 AND 3: *Que voyez-vous dans le tableau numéro 2? Dans le tableau numéro 2, je vois un chat.*

WOMAN 2: The whole class repeats each sentence which the professor enunciates, and each sentence echoes in your ears like a drumbeat.

CHORUS OF WOMEN 1 AND 3: *Que voyez-vous dans le tableau numéro 3? Dans le tableau numéro 3, je vois un arbre.*

WOMAN 2: And yet, already, unconsciously, you are searching for some other place, a place far from the group, all the while your mouth enunciating the words which the group enunciates, as you give up control momentarily and do what the others do.

CHORUS OF WOMEN 1 AND 3: *Que voyez-vous dans le tableau numéro 4? Dans le tableau numéro 4, je vois un garçon.*

WOMAN 2: Your mechanical participation soon turns to boredom, and boredom changes into the clouds of daydream, and now at the center of the clouds, the daydream becomes you, you are the clouds.

CHORUS OF WOMEN 1 AND 3: *Que voyez-vous dans le tableau numéro 4? Dans le tableau numéro 4, je vois …*

WOMAN 2: Imperceptibly, your voice ceases to resonate with the other voices. Soon you are far from the group. Soon you are in some other place, far, far from the group …

CHORUS OF WOMEN 1 AND 3: *Que voyez-vous dans le tableau numéro 5? Dans le tableau numéro 5, je vois …*

WOMAN 2: Now you are looking at the green trees outside, a very tender green, they seem to be waving to you, and you are mouthing the words as you watch the trees through the classroom window, as you watch the spring which has no use for words.

CHORUS OF WOMEN 1 AND 3: *Que voyez-vous dans le tableau numéro 6? Dans le tableau numéro 6, je vois une fille.*

WOMAN 2: Now your mind mounts the spring and gallops away, in search of peat moss, the cool shade of the woods, and adulterated odors, the fresh smell of mint mingled with the pungent smell of wild garlic, filling the air around you, emanating from the maddening grass, at the foot of the trees, beneath the moss.

CHORUS OF WOMEN 1 AND 3: *Que voyez-vous dans le tableau numéro 7? Dans le tableau numéro 7, je vois ...*

WOMAN 2: Your mind is an earthworm, penetrating the soil, and cradled in the roots of wild mint and garlic, the roots of the trees.
Your mind is the branch banging against the glass of the window.
Your mind is the tender green of the translucent leaf, the source of the penetrating light that makes the leaf translucent.

CHORUS OF WOMEN 1 AND 3: *Que voyez-vous dans le tableau numéro 8? Dans le tableau numéro 8, je vois le ciel.*

WOMAN 2: You are somewhere else. You no longer walk on the beaten path.
You are the branch, you are the leaf, you are the spring, you are the clouds. You are the tree.

CHORUS OF WOMEN 1 AND 3: *Que voyez-vous dans le tableau numéro 9? Dans le tableau numéro 9, je vois ...*

WOMAN 2: The cloud is you, you are the cloud. You are the mist. And the delicate, the divine drops that fall from the cloud, a rain so fine unhinges your mind.

CHORUS OF WOMEN 1 AND 3: *Que voyez-vous dans le tableau numéro 10? Dans le tableau numéro 10, je vois un nuage.*

WOMAN 2: Now there is nothing to hold back your hand, your right hand, so dexterous, from climbing, climbing up from beneath the desk, slinking up your thigh and stopping at your vagina. Up and up, there it is, your vagina, with its convex folds. And your hand lingers. The slightest pressure applied on the spot tells you this is a good spot. You just have to rub the clitoris, here, to glimpse the promise of a pleasure that was inconceivable before now, a pleasure that had been kept hidden from you. And while the mist from the cloud grows denser and whiter, there emanates from between your thighs an unknown heat, so powerful, so surprising for such a high cloud, that your thighs begin to tremble.

Now the cloud that you are is carried away, driven by a violent wind coming from the bottom of your cranium and passing along the spinal column to your pelvis. It comes without warning. It dazzles you and everything goes white, I swear, a total white-out, even with your eyes closed all is white. It pries your mouth open, dazzles your vocal chords, sends shockwaves down your thighs, and arches your back. You are ravished.

Your cheeks are red now. This spring is pretty hot, you know, and it dumps you back in the classroom because it doesn't care and because it is fleeting.

Now the cloud has dissipated.

Your eyes had a vague look in them a few moments ago, and now they focus once again on the French professor still parading about. *(Silence.)*

Que voyez-vous dans le tableau numéro 18?

Dans le tableau numéro 18, je vois … Je vois nothing at all.

Je vois a class room, during the day, 4 o'clock.

I saw myself there … I was ten years old when I discovered … *(Silence.)*

WOMAN 3 *(To WOMAN 2)*: Did I hear you say … masturbation?

WOMAN 2 *(To WOMAN 3)*: … masturbation … I didn't say … masturbation … Did I? Maybe I did … But she said it first! *(Pointing to WOMAN 1.)*

WOMAN 1: Oh did I?

WOMAN 2 *(To WOMAN 1)*: Well I'm sorry, but it seems to me that … you … you said masturbation … You even said: *masturbation*, like that. That is how you said it: *masturbation*, like that. That's how you said it.

WOMAN 1 *(To WOMAN 2)*: I don't understand. I did not say: *masturbation*, like that. I said: *masturbation*, that's all. Listen to how I'm saying it: *masturbation*. That's all. I said: *masturbation*, that's all.

WOMAN 2: You most certainly did not, you said: *masturbation*. And that is how you said it: *masturbation*! Like that, that is exactly how you said it: *masturbation*!

WOMAN 1: No, no, no. I beg your pardon, I did not say it how you say I said it. I'm saying that I said: *masturbation*, like that, because that is how I say it. Do you hear: *masturbation*! *Masturbation*! *Masturbation*!

WOMAN 2 *(After a silent pause)*: Well, alright … if you say so … *(Silence.)*

WOMAN 3: …When my husband and I have relations …

WOMAN 2: … I'm listening …

WOMAN 1 *(To WOMAN 2)*: … Bitch …

WOMAN 3: … we always turn out the lights. *(Silence.)*

WOMAN 1: Right …

WOMAN 2: You do?

WOMAN 3: Always. *(Silence.)*
I can't stand the thought of him seeing "it." *(Silence.)*
I would be mortified. *(Silence.)*
Besides, he's never seen "it." *(Silence.)*
The very thought that he might one day see "it," I can't stand it. *(Silence.)*
But there's a good reason: I simply don't find "it" beautiful.
That's all. I just prefer that he not see "it." *(Silence.)*
How dreadful if he did. *(Silence.)*
And why is that, I ask you, why? *(Silence.)*

Simply because "it" is not pretty, esthetically speaking. *(Silence.)*

Let's not kid ourselves: there must be a reason why "it" has been hidden from view all this time. For centuries and centuries. *(WOMAN 3 grabs a shovel and bit by bit begins digging a ditch.)*

Look at this Hermes statue, or this discus thrower, or this Olympian Apollo: the erectile plumbing is graceful, and the supporting package is appropriate.

But a woman, not one slit or triangle or hair sculpted to represent "it." The Venus de Milo, the Victory of Samothrace, all of them hide "it" behind their veils. And when they are nude, there is nothing between their legs, only a desert.

They will have none of "it." No hair, no slit, none of "it." Marble knows how to keep a secret. And it's just as well. Why else would "it" be so hard to get at?

And why does no one ever talk about "it"?

Except for perverts. And doctors, of course,

But that's different, unless your doctor is a pervert … *(Silence.)*

There are plenty of good reasons.

No, really, "it" is this I don't know what sort of thingy … it's formless.

No, really, I will spare you the nasty details … the … and those … and the …

Anyway. *(Silence.)*

No, really. *(Silence.)*

It's just so ugly, that's all.

No, really, look at beautiful things, I don't know, bees butterflies gardens … *(Silence.)*

Yes look at nature personally I love to garden and look at nature all day my roses my lilacs my hydrangea bushes I plant trees it's my secret garden my very own no one else's all mine and my husband is always saying who are you digging that new hole for dear he's always joking he's so funny tell me he says is it a chestnut, a magnolia, or a birch?

Did you know that for chestnut, magnolia, and birch trees you have to space the holes a certain distance apart to accommodate the roots of the cypresses in the hedge and to protect the rose bushes from frost you have to put compost or straw in the bottom of the hole. *(Silence.)* And in gopher holes you put sulfur to exterminate the nasty creatures. Ugh! *(She is still digging, faster and faster. The hole is getting deeper and deeper.)*

CHORUS OF WOMEN 1 AND 2: Hole.

WOMAN 3: Animals don't make such a fuss about "it," do they. To them "it" just seems natural.

CHORUS OF WOMEN 1 AND 2: Hole.

WOMAN 3: Animals clean "it" the same way they lick their paws or whiskers.

CHORUS OF WOMEN 1 AND 2: Hole-hole.

WOMAN 3: "It" doesn't bother them. They don't make a big deal of "it."

CHORUS OF WOMEN 1 AND 2: Hole-hole-hole.

WOMAN 3: No, I don't have time to reflect on "it." When I get ready in the morning, I take a shower and clean "it" the way I would use soap on a … dish or plate. All very natural. I rinse, I'm done. "It" is clean, I'm happy. Great.

CHORUS OF WOMEN 1 AND 2: Hole-hole.

WOMAN 3: When I take time to reflect, I reflect on other things, not on "it."

CHORUS OF WOMEN 1 AND 2: Hole.

WOMAN 3: Yes look at nature personally I love to garden and look at nature all day my roses my lilacs my hydrangea bushes I plant trees it's my secret garden my very own no one else's all mine and my husband is always saying who are you digging that new hole for dear he's always joking he's so funny tell me he says is it a chestnut, a magnolia, or a birch? *(Silence.)* Yes personally I love to garden.

CHORUS OF WOMEN 1 AND 2: Gopher hole.

WOMAN 3: My roses. My lilacs. My hydrangea bushes.

CHORUS OF WOMEN 1 AND 2: Pot hole.

WOMAN 3: Anything but "it." "It" is not my main preoccupation, and "it" never has been. I leave "it" to the care of my gynecologist. He knows much better than I do what he's talking about when he talks about "it." A reproductive organ, nothing more. At least animals have it figured out. Anyway, you can see I have no interest in "it." But what about this fascination with pornography?

CHORUS OF WOMEN 1 AND 2: Man hole.

WOMAN 3: Beyond a purely physiological and medical interest …

CHORUS OF WOMEN 1 AND 2: Pie hole.

WOMAN 3: I have no interest in "it."

CHORUS OF WOMEN 1 AND 2: Blow hole.

WOMAN 3: I mean, really, a hole, it's only a hole. And every hole is a vacuum.

CHORUS OF WOMEN 1 AND 2: Come hole.

WOMAN 3: And a vacuum is nothing.

CHORUS OF WOMEN 1 AND 2: Black hole.

WOMAN 3: No, really, what business do all these women have talking about … "it." Shame on you!

CHORUS OF WOMEN 1 AND 2: Black out.

WOMAN 3: You should be ashamed, for Heaven's sake!

CHORUS OF WOMEN 1 AND 2: Key hole.

WOMAN 3: Indeed it amounts to nothing more than pure voyeurism!

CHORUS OF WOMEN 1 AND 2: Spy hole.

WOMAN 3: As if "it" were the path to self-knowledge! Outrageous.

CHORUS OF WOMEN 1 AND 2: Worm hole.

WOMAN 3: The society we live in makes no sense.

CHORUS OF WOMEN 1 AND 2: Butt hole.

WOMAN 3: We have forgotten about nature.

CHORUS OF WOMEN 1 AND 2: Loop hole.

WOMAN 3: No, really, take a good look at nature. Why don't we dig holes and plant trees! Now there's a useful occupation. Yes! Start digging! *(She has now disappeared completely in the hole she has been digging. In a moment, however, we hear her whispering down there.)*

It … It's true … When I have relations with my husband … we always turn out the lights. Always. I can't stand the thought of him seeing "it." I would be mortified.

Besides, he's never seen "it." The very thought that he might one day see "it," I can't stand it. But there's a good reason: I simply don't find "it" beautiful.

I just prefer that he not see "it." How dreadful if he did.

And why is that, I ask you, why?

Simply because "it" is not pretty, esthetically speaking. Let's not kid ourselves: there must be a reason why "it" has been hidden from view all this time. For centuries and centuries. No, really, look at beautiful things, I don't know, bees butterflies gardens … Yes look at nature personally I love to garden and look at nature all day my roses my lilacs my hydrangea bushes I plant trees it's my secret garden my very own no one else's all mine and my husband is always saying who are you digging that new hole for dear he's always joking he's so funny tell me he says is it a chestnut, a magnolia, or a birch? When I have relations with my husband, I couldn't stand the thought of him seeing "it" but there's a good reason I just prefer that he not see "it" key hole how dreadful if he did pie hole "it" is simply not pretty, esthetically speaking man hole I prefer nature gofer hole there's a useful occupation worm hole there must be a reason why "it" has been hidden from view come hole so hard to get at black hole we never speak of "it" black hole no really I don't what sort of thingy black hole yes look at nature personally I love to garden …

WOMAN 2 *(Interrupting WOMAN 3)*: Who are you digging that new hole for dear? *(Silence.)*

WOMAN 3: It's true, I just love to garden … *(Silence.)*

WOMAN 1: I went to Kmart yesterday …

WOMAN 3: My roses my lilacs my hydrangea bushes …

WOMAN 1: … to buy … something sexy and frilly … *(Silence.)* … something frivolous, a little something, nothing special.

WOMAN 3: Planting trees …

WOMAN 1: My Bernie, you know, he loves …

WOMAN 3: … Planting trees …

WOMAN 1: I love my Bernie … *(Silence.)*

When Bernie comes over, I go all—well, I … I want to look pretty. Yes, I go all out for Bernie … He doesn't come over that often, so … when he does, it's a treat. I went to Kmart to buy … something sexy and frilly … something frivolous, a little something, nothing special. I know what Bernie likes. I like it too. I always tell him Bernie you dog you scoundrel you good-for-nothing. Bad boy, I say, my man, love of my life. And when he sees the little sexy frivolous frills I bought at the store, he laughs then softly he says: you're like a dream come true.

WOMAN 3: Who are you digging that new hole for dear?

WOMAN 2: For you my darling for you.
For your eyes and for your hands, and the nape of your neck, and your chest and your earlobes and your lips and your butt.

WOMAN 3: Who are you digging that new hole for dear?

WOMAN 2 *(Jumping out of a hole)*: For you my darling for you.
For your toes and the stubble on your chin and your musky smell and your rebel mouth.

WOMAN 3: Who are you digging that new hole for dear?

WOMAN 1: For you my darling for you.
For the shape of your hands, the color of your skin, for your belly-button and your big nose and your butt.

WOMAN 3: For you my darling for you.
My silk bra, my satin panties, my lace corset …

WOMAN 2: My elastic thong.

WOMAN 1: For you my darling for you.

WOMAN 3: My nylons, my silk garters, my tulle chemise, my thigh-highs …

WOMAN 2: My elastic thong.

WOMAN 1: For you my darling for you.

WOMAN 3: My micro fiber push-up bra, my sheer nighty, my garter belt, my mules …

WOMAN 2: My elastic thong.

WOMAN 1: For you my darling for you.

CHORUS OF WOMEN: My spike heels,
My snake-skin panties,
My crocodile miniskirt,
My fur coat,
My horsehair boots,
My Louis Vuitton knock-off,
My designer suit,
And my little black dress!

WOMAN 2: My elastic thong!

WOMAN 1: For you my darling for you.

WOMAN 2: Come, come here, watch this.

WOMAN 3: I want to see him drool, like a dog.

WOMAN 1: In rut.

WOMAN 2: A hunting dog.

WOMAN 3: In hot pursuit.

WOMAN 1: Come here, on your knees.

WOMAN 2: Make him crawl on his knees.

WOMAN 3: Make him drool, the dog.

WOMAN 1: Make him beg.

CHORUS OF WOMEN: Make him drool, the dog.
Make him beg, the dog.
Make him crawl, make him come.

WOMAN 2: My silk bra, my satin panties, my lace corset ...

WOMAN 1: Oh Bernie ...

WOMAN 2: My elastic thong.

WOMAN 3: My nylons, my silk garters, my tulle chemise, my thigh-highs ...

WOMAN 2: My elastic thong.

WOMAN 3: My micro fiber push-up bra, my sheer nighty, my garter belt, my mules ...

WOMAN 1: Oh Bernie ...

WOMAN 2: My elastic thong.

CHORUS OF WOMEN: My spike heels,
My snake-skin panties,
My crocodile miniskirt,
My fur coat,
My horsehair boots,
My Louis Vuitton knock-off,
My designer suit,
And my little black dress!

WOMAN 2: My elastic thong!

WOMAN 1: For you my darling for you, I go all out for you, I want you to die before, I want you to weep on my cunt …

WOMAN 3: For you my darling for you.

WOMAN 2: My elastic thong.

WOMAN 1: When Bernie comes over, I go all, well, I … I want to look pretty. Yes, I go all out for Bernie … He doesn't come over all that often, so … when he does, it's a treat. I went to Kmart to buy … something sexy and frilly … something frivolous, a little something, nothing special. I know what Bernie likes. I like it too. I always tell him Bernie you dog you scoundrel you good-for-nothing. Bad boy, I say, my man, love of my life. And when he sees the little sexy frivolous frills I bought at the store, he laughs then softly he says: you're like a dream come true. You are the sea and I sail and you are the salty spray and the foam that peppers the rocks. That's the way you are.

WOMAN 2: My elastic thong.

WOMAN 1: That's the way I am. I am the salty spray and the foam that peppers the rocks. I have a taste like the sea. I taste of brine, seagulls, algae. I am a seashell pungent with ocean smells. I have a taste like the sea.

WOMAN 2: My elastic thong.

Each woman takes up the refrain, then the CHORUS OF WOMEN, *several times, as they rock left and right as on a ship.*

CHORUS OF WOMEN: That's the way I am. I am the salty spray and the foam that peppers the rocks. I have a taste like the sea. I taste of brine, seagulls, algae. I am a sea shell pungent with ocean smells. I have a taste like the sea. That's the way I am. I am the salty spray and the foam that peppers the rocks. I have a taste like the sea. I taste of brine, seagulls, algae. I am a sea shell pungent with ocean smells. I have a taste like the sea.

WOMAN 2: My elastic thong.

WOMAN 1: Oh Bernie, come oh come … When Bernie comes … to the house. *Togliti la mutandina …*

WOMAN 2 *(Interpreting WOMAN 1's Italian into English)*: Take off your panties!

WOMAN 1: *Togila tu la mutandina!*

WOMAN 2: Take my panties off yourself!

WOMAN 1: *Non ci arrivo. Non mi riesca taglierla con i bluejeans!*

WOMAN 2: I can't get them off. I can't get them off with your bluejeans.

WOMAN 1: *Va bene, aspetta.*

WOMAN 2: OK, wait a minute.

WOMAN 1: *Oh qui qui no. Oh si, muoviti.*

WOMAN 2: For cryin' out, no. Oh yes. Faster.

WOMAN 1: *Aspetta! Aspetta! Vai troppo veloce!*

WOMAN 2: Wait! Wait a minute. You're going too fast.

WOMAN 1: *Ma é la tua cintura. Che cosé queta fibbia da cretini. Non riesco a slacciarla, 'sta fibbia del cazza!*

WOMAN 2: But your belt. What is this stupid belt buckle? I can't get this belt buckle off.

WOMAN 1: *Aspetta! Aspetta! Ecco qua!*

WOMAN 2: Hold it! Wait! Got it!

WOMAN 1: *Madre Santissima! Muio!*

WOMAN 2: Holy Mother of God! I'm dying!

WOMAN 1: *Ah qui qui non mi tocare piu, aspetta!*

WOMAN 2: Oh, ow, get off me! Wait!

WOMAN 1: *Oh no, non posso. Oh troppo troppo bello!*

WOMAN 2: Oh no, I can't. It's so beautiful!

WOMAN 1: *Aïe! Mi fai male! Fai attenzione!*

WOMAN 2: Ouch! You're hurting me! Watch out!

WOMAN 1: *Ta cerniera! Fai attenzione all cerniera lompo!*

WOMAN 2: Your zipper! Watch your zipper!

WOMAN 1: *Madre Santissima é troppo! Muoio, oh si muoio ora!*

WOMAN 2: Mother of God that is good! I'm dying, I'm gonna come!

WOMAN 1: *Oh non, non subito! Non morire ora!*

WOMAN 2: Not right now! Don't come yet!

WOMAN 1: *Oh si, non, non moriro subito, non subito. Amore mio, amore, amore mio!*

WOMAN 2: Yes, wait, no, I won't come yet, not yet. My love, oh love, my love.

WOMAN 1: *Cosi, cosi é, sei, il, mio … io … tu … te …*

WOMAN 2: That's it, that … You're my … I …You …

WOMAN 3 *(Once again in English, no more interpreter)*: Don't love me. Don't look at me. Don't want me. Don't ask me.

CHORUS OF WOMEN 1 AND 2: Come oh come

WOMAN 3: Don't touch me. Don't kiss me. Don't tell me.

CHORUS OF WOMEN 1 AND 2: Come oh come

WOMAN 3: Don't bug me. Don't provoke me. Don't tease me.

CHORUS OF WOMEN 1 AND 2: Come oh come

WOMAN 3: Don't fuck me. Don't screw me. Don't poke me. Don't do me.

CHORUS OF WOMEN 1 AND 2: Come oh come

WOMAN 3: It's not working. It's not gonna work like that. Let's try something else. We just have to count to … *(Silence.)* Don't love me.

CHORUS OF WOMEN 1 AND 2: Even if it means I count

WOMAN 3: Don't love me.

CHORUS OF WOMEN 1 AND 2: Even if it means you count on me

WOMAN 3: Don't love me

CHORUS OF WOMEN 1 AND 2: Even if it means you count

WOMAN 3: Don't love me. It's not working. It's not gonna work like that. Let's try something else. We just have to count to …

Chorus of Women 1 and 2: What number do we start with?

Woman 3: Start with one. Start counting. You go one, I go two, together we go three.

Chorus of Women 1 and 2: Come oh come I forget the world with you

Woman 3: Don't love me.

Chorus of Women 1 and 2: Come oh come I forget myself with you

Woman 3: Don't love me.

Chorus of Women 1 and 2: Come oh come make me forget in your arms

Woman 3: Don't love me.

Chorus of Women 1 and 2: Come and go I forget the world with you

Woman 3: Don't love me.

Chorus of Women 1 and 2: Come and go I forget myself with you

Woman 3: Don't love me.

Chorus of Women 1 and 2: Come and go make me forget in your arms

Woman 3: Don't love me. It's not working. It's not gonna work like that. Let's try something else. We just have to count to …

Chorus of Women 1 and 2: Three

Woman 3: One

Chorus of Women 1 and 2: Two

Woman 3: Love me, want me, ask me, see me

Chorus of Women 1 and 2: One, two, three

Woman 3: Love me, touch me, kiss me, tell me

Chorus of Women 1 and 2: One, two, three

Woman 3: Love me, provoke me, tease me, fuck me

Chorus of Women 1 and 2: One, two, three

Woman 3: Love me, screw me, poke me, do me

Chorus of Women 1 and 2: Come oh come I forget the world with you

Woman 3: Come and go

Chorus of Women 1 and 2: Come oh come I forget myself with you

Woman 3: Come and go

Chorus of Women 1 and 2: Come oh come make me forget in your arms

Woman 3: Come and go

Chorus of Women 1 and 2: Come oh come

Woman 3: No. Not now. Not yet. *(Silence.)*
Come and go I forget the world with you
Come and go I forget myself with you
Come make me forget in your arms
And go *(Silence.)*

WOMAN 2: So … Did you come? he goes. Did you come? I'm like: no. I shook my head: "no", and my mouth said: "No."

So you didn't come? I'm like: well, no, you can see, can't you, no. I didn't … come. But it doesn't matter, sweetie. I mean I did say: it doesn't matter, sweetie. *(Silence.)*

Well, because I thought … he's like: because you went UH-UH, I thought … that you came … I thought. I'm like: no, I just said I didn't, you can see can't you, I didn't. And I didn't say anything and neither did he.

And there was this horrible silence and no one said anything. *(Silence.)*

Later on he's like: OK. I'm like: no, wait. He's like: you are happy? I mean, except for that, we're OK … right? I'm like: yes. Sweetie! yes, I'm happy. He's like: OK, and I'm like: OK. And then I said good night sweetie and turned out the light. I'm like: good night. OK.

And there was this horrible silence and no one said anything. *(Silence.)*

WOMAN 3: And then … You shouldn't have turned off the light, angel. I'm like: what? The light, why did you turn it off? Please turn it back on, angel, I love you. He slips that in: I love you. I'm like: you know … I have to wake up early tomorrow. I know, angel, please turn the light back on, please. I'm like: sweetie, no one is to blame here. No one. He's like: I know, angel, please turn the light back on.

So I turned the light back on. *(Silence.)*

After a while, I'm like: sweetheart, I am very tired and I … The whole thing is my fault, he says, dead serious. I'm like totally non-chalant, I'm like: sweetheart! No, absolutely not. But of course he says: you refuse to admit it but I have proof. You always go UH-UH even though nothing's happening, which means you're faking it when you go …

CHORUS OF WOMEN: UH-UH

WOMAN 2: … because you don't want to make me feel bad, but in fact you and your …

CHORUS OF WOMEN: UH-UH

WOMAN 2: … are having the opposite effect. I can't believe it, all this nonsense and for what … goddamn shit, I can't believe we're fighting over this shit, a stupid fuck …

I'm like: there's no need to get upset … Or to use that language. Really. It's pointless. And there was this horrible silence and no one said anything. *(Silence.)*

So now again, he's like: OK. I'm like: no, wait. He's like: you are happy? I mean, except for that, we're OK … right? I'm like: listen, it's hard to explain. He's like: I'm listening, I'm like: OK, listen. Here it is. When I go …

CHORUS OF WOMEN: … UH-UH …

WOMAN 2: … it's not some sort of act that I'm putting over on you by going …

CHORUS OF WOMEN: … UH-UH …

WOMAN 2: … so I can make you feel bad you idiot you're being a little paranoid don't you think …

CHORUS OF WOMEN: UH-UH

WOMAN 2: … and I'm not making fun of you or anything else I just love you and don't want you to feel responsible and in any case certain things do feel good you know …

WOMAN 1: Don't think I'm totally frigid and made of stone, what about my breasts, for example, and the hair on my head and the lobes of my ears and the palms of my hands and the toes on my feet and tips of my fingers and the lids of my eyes and the nape of my neck and the lips of my mouth I mean there's a whole package here not just a vagina and all of it is in perfect working order take my word for it and you shouldn't think that it's your fault and when I go UH-UH I'm being totally sincere I swear and sometimes also it feels good. Also. Sometimes. It feels good. *(Silence.)*

He's like: OK, we should sleep in separate beds. *(Silence.)* We should induce a state of … deprivation, a sort of dynamic incarceration. Yes, abstention. *(Silence.)*
I'm like: you mean abstinence. He's like: yes, abstinence.
That's ridiculous.
You're right, it's ridiculous. Maybe I'm going about it all wrong.
No, you're perfect.
I hate it when you say I'm perfect. What does that mean "perfect"? No one is "perfect."
Alright, then, you're very good. *(Silence.)* … Very good. … Well, pretty good.
Well that's not enough for me.
Well, sweetie, it's not enough for me either, but you don't see it keeping me awake at night now do you.
And I turned out the light because well I had had enough. *(Darkness and silence again.)*

WOMAN 2: Angel, don't I get a kiss?
Yes of course sweetie. *(We hear the smacking sound of a kiss.)*

WOMAN 2: White … white. Everything was white. White as snow. White as spring.
My dress, my train, white. My shoes, white.
My bouquet was white, and the flowers in my hair were roses.

CHORUS OF WOMEN: They were white roses, of course …

WOMAN 2: My veil, white, and the crinoline and my stockings, white.

CHORUS OF WOMEN: All our roses, white; all our trains, white; everything white, down to our shoes. All our bouquets, white; and the flowers in our hair, white roses, of course. All our veils, and the crinoline, white. And all our stockings, white.

WOMAN 2: My garter, my petticoat, white; my panties, white. Down to the smallest detail, white.

CHORUS OF WOMEN: All our petticoats, white; all our garters, white; all our panties, white; down to the smallest detail, white; white on the outside, white on the inside.

WOMAN 2: The flowers on the altar, white. White lilies.

CHORUS OF WOMEN: Of course ... White as a goose, white on the outside, white on the inside.

WOMAN 2: And the rice they threw at us, white.

CHORUS OF WOMEN: White rice, of course ... all white. White as a goose, white on the outside, white on the inside.

WOMAN 2: The table cloth, white; the bread, white; the leg of lamb with string beans, white.

CHORUS OF WOMEN: White string beans?

WOMAN 2: Of course ...

CHORUS OF WOMEN: And white rice, white, white, white.

WOMAN 2: Of course ...

CHORUS OF WOMEN: White as a goose, white on the inside, white on the outside.

WOMAN 2: And the waltz, white; the party favors, the wedding cake, the chocolate, white; and the wine they served, white.

CHORUS OF WOMEN: And white wine, white, white, white.

WOMAN 2: The party favors, the streamers, the confetti, white. And my dress spinning round, white.

CHORUS OF WOMEN: And white wine, more white wine.

WOMAN 2: My husband smiling, white; his teeth, white.

CHORUS OF WOMEN: And white wine, more white wine.

WOMAN 2: My dress spinning round, white; my veil, white; and springtime, white; and the waltz, white. White on the outside, white on the inside.

CHORUS OF WOMEN: Her dress spinning round, white … The springtime, white …
And white wine, more white wine.

WOMAN 2: My dress spinning round, white … The springtime, white …

CHORUS OF WOMEN: And white wine, more white wine.

WOMAN 2: Spinning round …

CHORUS OF WOMEN: And white wine, more white wine.

WOMAN 2: Spinning round …

CHORUS OF WOMEN: And white wine, more white wine.

WOMAN 2: Spinning round …

CHORUS OF WOMEN: And white wine, more white wine. WHITE!! *(Silence.)*

WOMAN 2: For the big night, a room. White.
In a big four-star hotel.
In the room, the bed for the big night: a big bed, all white.
Too much white wine, so he collapses right there, on the much-too-big bed.

He grew very white, grumbled, got out of bed, and headed teetering for the bathroom.

There he bent down, over the sink, and vomited. Long and hard, all the white wine.

It spilled everywhere, all of it, all over the white tiles, down to the least drop.

I didn't think it would ever stop.

Finally, when he was done, he collapsed next to the sink and started snoring.

I dragged him out of the bathroom, and he's a big man so it was no easy task, and put him to bed, the big white bed, and swaddled him like an infant.

Instantly, he started snoring again.

His cock just hung there more pathetic than my veil.

His pink cock, my white veil. *(Silence.)*

Then I decided to wash the white tiles and the sink and with an old hanger I managed to unblock the drain in the sink.

When I had finished, I sat on the white bed that was meant for the big night, just sat there, legs closed, vulva untouched, labia unopened, the inner folds disappearing into themselves, my clit untried, my cunt clean and white ...

And he went right on snoring. No change whatsoever.

I just sat there on my virgin-white ass, and I thought about my cherry.

Still snoring.

I thought about those people who say that a woman must keep her virginity intact.

Still snoring.

I thought about those cultures which display the bloody sheet the day after. The blood from the broken hymen proves that the bride was a virgin and that the marriage was consummated that very night ...

Still snoring, harder and louder.

And I thought, what a bunch of bullshit.

And so, sitting there on my virgin-white ass, my veil fallen like a meringue, I began to think ... very hard ... and the hotel receptionist came to mind....

When I left the room, he was still snoring on the big white bed that was

meant for the big night, snoring harder and louder, my beloved.
Excuse me, Mr. Receptionist of the four-star hotel meant for the big night ... Are you not asleep, sir?

The Receptionist: As receptionist and night watchman, I often partake of the celebrations. I love the night, madam, I love the white moonlight glimmering on my desk, I love the lonely women who cannot sleep, longing for the dawn, their honeymoon down the drain.
I am always awake, madam, and I am always at your service.
How may this night watchman four-star hotel receptionist who loves the glimmering moonlight and who loves to partake be of service to you , madam? Perhaps the service is not to madam's liking? Perhaps madam would like to be rid of something that weighs on her, something that causes such a fuss ...Very good, madam. Which room? *(Silence.)*

Woman 1: He used to say: the faculty for self-abnegation which you women possess is amazing.

Woman 3: They say: if my aunt wore the pants, she would be my uncle.

Woman 1: He used to say: I have often seen the faculty for self-abnegation which you women possess in the eyes of my mother.

Woman 2: They say: they're all sluts, except mom.

Woman 1: He used to say: self-abnegation, emphasizing the guttural, against the back of his throat, like this: self-abnegation. That's how he used to say it.

Woman 3: They say: your mother is so ugly she has teeth in her crotch.

Woman 1: He used to say: self-abnegation, self-abne*ga*tion, like he was choking on it.

Woman 2: They say: Hell hath no fury like a woman scorned.

WOMAN 1: He used to say: "Her self-abnegation was amazing," and he would choke on his adoration, he worshiped his mother like a holy icon, he sang her praises to the skies.

WOMAN 3: They say: do not let the beauty of woman take you, nor become enamored of her.

WOMAN 1: He used to say: do you realize, my mother raised eight children.

WOMAN 2: They say: woman is the root of all evil, and she is the cause of death.

WOMAN 1: He used to say: do you realize, my mother quit her studies to raise us.

WOMAN 3: They say: a woman who keeps silence is a gift from the Lord, and priceless is she who is gracious and well taught.

WOMAN 1: He used to say: do you realize, my mother always served the father, and never a word from her, never a word.

WOMAN 2: They say: do not give yourself to a woman, lest she establish ascendancy over you.

WOMAN 1: He used to say: and yet, it was no walk in the park, serving the father. Papa was no joker.

WOMAN 3: They say: strike your wife, though you know not why, for she most certainly does.

They say: do not give yourself to a woman, lest she establish ascendancy over you.

WOMAN 1: He used to say: the self-abnegation for which you women are so admirably fitted from birth can be explained by your sex organ, its very configuration and morphology demonstrate that you are passive creatures, destined to suffer whatever is thrust on you. Is that not why you are called the "weaker" sex? *(Silence.)*

He used to say: the faculty for self-abnegation which you women possess is amazing. I have often seen the faculty for self-abnegation which you women possess in the eyes of my mother. He used to say: self-abnegation, emphasizing the guttural, against the back of his throat, like this: self-abnegation. That's how he used to say it. "Her self-abnegation was amazing" and he would choke on his adoration, he worshiped his mother like a holy icon, he sang her praises to the skies. Do you realize, my mother raised eight children. Do you realize, my mother quit her studies to raise us. Do you realize, my mother always served the father, and never a word from her, never a word. And yet, it was no walk in the park, serving the father. Papa was no joker. *(Silence.)*

All that time I just kept my mouth shut, not a peep. I was waiting for him to finish.

He used to say: the self-abnegation for which you women are so admirably fitted from birth can be explained by your sex organ, its very configuration and morphology demonstrate that you are passive creatures, destined to suffer whatever is thrust on you. Is that not why you are called the "weaker" sex?

While he finished, I would look for a cool spot on the floor, to place my cheek on, to soothe the burning sensation he always left me with.

Self-abnegation, he used to say, emphasizing the guttural.

WOMAN 2: They say … so many things, don't they. *(Silence.)*

WOMAN 3: Cock is not human. She says. Those were her exact words.

It's not human. Cock is a war machine. Look at these war zones. Look. Just look at them.

Cock is not human.

I have blood on my hands, I said. Look, I told her, I have blood on my hands, but she wasn't listening.

Cock is not human. She says. Those were her exact words.

It's not human. Cock violates women. Look at these violated women. Look. Just look at them.

Cock is not human.

I have blood on my hands, I said. Look, I told her, I have blood on my hands, but she wasn't listening.

Cock is not human. She says. Those were her exact words.
It's not human. Cock violates children. Look at those children. Look. Just look at them.
Cock is not human.

I have blood on my hands, I said. Look, I told her, I have blood on my hands, but she wasn't listening.

Cock is not human. She says. Those were her exact words.
It's not human. Cock marches in lockstep, Cock invents the concentration camps. Look, just look at the barbed wire.
Cock is not human.

I have blood on my hands, I said, and the sons who sprang from our wombs yesterday were not all like that, and the sons who will spring from our wombs tomorrow will not all be like that.

But the majority, she said, the majority of our sons take that path. Now raise your hands. She said. Now raise your hands.

I have blood on my hands, I said. I, too, have blood on my hands. And then no one said another word. *(Silence.)*

WOMAN 2: You are dead.
They lowered you in the ground today.
And my pubic hair turned all white.
My pubic hair is white, from the shock.
Damn, I had no idea that fear and time and loss could whiten my hair down there. I had no idea.
I thought about dying them. You know, the way I have dyed the hair on my head since my 30th birthday. I thought about dying my pubic hair.

But what for, and for who?

Now I know: I will never have another man inside me. Never another penis inside me.

I know that now. I know it. You were it.

You are dead.

They lowered you in the ground today.

And they buried you with dirt and my sex shed a final tear for the last shovel of dirt. A final tear, for you, my sex.

And then, afterwards, it just dried up.

Damn, I had no idea that fear and time and loss could turn a vagina into a desert.

I had no idea.

I thought of making it wet again, you know the way you've always done since we fell in love.

But what for, and for who?

Now I know: when I itch down there, I will raise up my eyes and see you in the sky. I know. Then you will become my fantasy, my pure fantasy. You will be up in the sky, with two big white wings and a huge cock, a huge pink cock, so beautiful, that only looking at it will make me come.

Now I know: there will never be another man in me. Never another penis in me.

I know that now. I know it. You were it.

You are dead.

They lowered you in the ground today.

And when they closed up the hole, my sex closed up.

White from the shock, dry as a desert, smooth as an arm.

That's it.

Now I know: there will never be another man in me. Never another penis in me.

I know that now. I know it. You were it.

You are dead.

They lowered you in the ground today. *(Silence, then softly.)*

Push … Push, ladies … Push …

WOMAN 1: The world screams as it exits my womb. The world cries. The world is nothing but screaming and crying.

CHORUS OF WOMEN 2 AND 3: Push … Push, ladies … Push …

WOMAN 1: There is blood everywhere. I hold tight to the stirrups. The world bleeds. The world is nothing but bleeding.

CHORUS OF WOMEN 2 AND 3: Push … Push, ladies … Push …
The world weeps as it exits my womb. The world sobs. The world is nothing but weeping and sobbing.
Push … Push, ladies … Push …

WOMAN 1: The world exits my womb. The world is broken. The world has broken me.

CHORUS OF WOMEN 2 AND 3: Push … Push, ladies … Push …

WOMAN 1: Finally the world quiets down. In my arms the world at last grows calm.
The world … A taste of milk. *(Silence, then all three women up front.)*
I have never had a problem with … sex …

WOMAN 2: I have never had a problem with … sex …

WOMAN 3: I have never had a problem with … sex …

WOMAN 2: Sex is something totally natural to me.

WOMAN 3: Something free of problems.

WOMAN 1: I am normal. In terms of sex also. I am normal. I have never been raped, and I have never been a victim of incest.

WOMAN 2: At my house, we used to talk about sex in a very natural way.

WOMAN 3: I learned about the birds and the bees at a very young age. And I've known some wonderful men. Perfect gentlemen. Lovely.

WOMAN 1: I have deeply loved several men. They were never disrespectful in any way. We always found the time to talk.

WOMAN 2: I am a woman … a liberated woman. I work. I love my work. And I'm not stressed out. My work is a blast.

WOMAN 3: I don't have any children. … Maybe some day. Maybe with him. I think he will make a good father.

WOMAN 1: I am a Western woman.

WOMAN 2: I am a Western woman.

WOMAN 3: I am a Western woman.

WOMAN 1: A liberated woman …

WOMAN 2: A liberated woman …

WOMAN 3: A liberated woman …

WOMAN 1: From a run-of-the-mill neighborhood …

WOMAN 2: From a run-of-the-mill neighborhood …

WOMAN 3: From a run-of-the-mill neighborhood …

WOMAN 1: In a well-functioning society …

WOMAN 2: In a well-functioning society …

WOMAN 3: In a well-functioning society … I believe

Woman 1: … I believe …

Woman 2: … I believe …

Woman 3: Yes, I believe that … I am a woman … a happy woman.

Woman 2: Yes, I believe that …

Woman 3: … I am happy.

Woman 2: Yes. … I believe that … all is well.

Woman 3: All is well …

Woman 1: Ladies, I have to close up now. They have already put the chairs on the tables upstairs and cleaned the bar and the terrace. I also have to count the register, ladies, and put away my mops and turn out the lights.

Woman 2: Good-bye, dear.

Woman 3: Good-bye.

Woman 1: Ladies, please don't forget … my cup. *(Chorus of Women 2 and 3 place tips in the cup.)*

Woman 2: The price of my sex.

Woman 3: The price of my sex.

Woman 1: It's my secret joy.

Woman 2: It's my secret joy.

Woman 3: It's … my secret … joy.

CHORUS OF ALL THREE WOMEN *(Whispering)*: It's … our … secret …

The CHORUS OF WOMEN exit. Lights out. Black.

Translation commissioned by Urban Gypsy Productions, New York, thanks to a grant from the Association Beaumarchais, Paris.

Biographies

Guy Bennett (translator, *Adramelech's Monologue*) is a poet/translator and author of four books, his collection of poetry *Drive to Cluster* among them. He is the publisher of Seeing Eye Books, co-editor of Seismicity Editions, and a contributing editor to the *New Review of Literature*. He lives in Los Angeles and is Associate Professor at Otis College of Art and Design.

Olivier Cadiot (playwright, *A.W.O.L.*) was born in Paris in 1956. His first book of poetry, *L'art poetic,* was published by Editions P.O.L. in 1988. This was followed by several short plays for the composer Pascal Dusapin and an adaptation for the opera *Romeo & Juliette*. In 1993, Cadiot published his poetic text *Futur, ancien, fugitif* and wrote his first full-length play *Soeurs et frères* for the director Ludovic Lagarde, with whom he has enjoyed an enduring partnership ever since. Lagarde adapted Cadiot's novel *Le Colonel des zouaves* as a theatrical monologue in 1997, *Le Retour définitif et durable de l'être aimé* (2002), and *Fairy Queen* (2004) for the Théâtre National de la Colline in Paris. Cadiot has also realized a number of music projects with contemporary composers Georges Aperghis, Gilles Grand, and others.

Emmanuelle Marie (playwright, *Cut*) was born in 1965, in Boulogne sur Mer. An actress and playwright, she studied modern literature and film at the University of Lille and co-founded the Compagnie des Docks in Boulogne sur Mer with director Jacques Descorde. Her plays include *Ecce homo?* and *Avant la chute.* In 2000, her first novel *Le Paradis des tortues* was pre-selected for *Elle* magazine's Women Readers' Prize as well as the Chambery's Festival of First Novels Prize. In May 2001, she wrote *Cut*, which premiered at the Passerelles Theatre in Montreuil-sur-Mer and played at the Théâtre du Rond-Point in June 2003, directed by Jacques Descorde. Her play *Blanc* premiered at the Théâtre de la Madeleine in Paris in fall 2006. She died on May 10, 2007.

Philippe Minyana (playwright, *Inventories*) was born in Besançon in 1946. Minyana pursued a teaching career while studying acting at the Conservatoire d'Art Dramatique. His first play, *Les dimanches blancs*, appeared in 1978. Since then he has written over 35 plays which have been widely produced, published, broadcast on radio, translated, and staged abroad. His plays *Chambres* and *Inventaires* have been included in the theatre studies program for the baccalauréat exam. In 2000 Philippe Minyana became co-director with Robert Cantarella of the Théâtre Dijon-Bourgogne, and later associate playwright at Théâtre Ouvert (Paris). His play *La Maison des Morts* premiered at the Comédie Française in February 2006, and his most recent plays, *Histoire de Roberta* and *Ca Va*, were published by Editions Théâtrales.

Valère Novarina (playwright, *Adramelech's Monologue*), dramatist, director, stage designer, painter, and performance artist, was born in 1947 in Switzerland. He studied philosophy, philology, and theatre history at the Sorbonne in Paris. His first play *L'atelier volant* was staged by Jean-Pierre Sarrazac at the Théâtre Jean Vilar, in Suresnes. In 1978, he began publishing his work: "utopian theatre," "poetic" plays, novels adapted for the stage with multiple characters, and theoretical works which explore the actor's body. In 1986, he began staging some of his own works, drawing the characters, and painting the sets. These include *Vous qui habitez le temps*, *Je suis*, *La Chair de l'homme,* and *Le Jardin de reconnaissance.*

José Pliya (playwright, *We Were Sitting on the Shores of the World ...*) was born in Cotonou, Benin, West Africa in 1966. Playwright, actor, director, and teacher, he holds a doctorate in Modern Literature from the University of Lille, where he also taught. Artistic director of Ecritures Théâtrales Contemporaines en Caraibe (Contemporary Caribbean Playwriting) and former director of the Alliances françaises of Dominica and Cameroon, Pliya is the author of numerous plays, several of them published by L'Avant-Scène théâtre, Collection des Quatre Vents. His plays have been produced in major French theatres such as La Comédie Française, the Théâtre National de Chaillot, the Théâtre de l'oeuvre, the Théâtre du Rond-Point Champs Elysées, and the Lucernaire theatre. In 2005, José Pliya was appointed artistic director of l'Archipel, the National Theatre of Guadeloupe, French West Indies.

Marion Shoevaert (adaptation, *A. W.O.L.*), director, producer, and translator, is a founding member of In Parentheses Inc. She adapted Cole Swensen's translation *Colonel Zoo* as *A. W.O.L.,* which she produced as part of the Act French festival, at the 59E59 Theater in 2005.

Michèle Sigal (playwright, *Pumpkin on the Air*) was born in 1952 in Ay-Champagne, France, and studied literature and acting. She is the author of seven plays, which include *Les Flambants, Les Stagnants, L'Heure bleue, Gémonies, une Antigone, Belinda morte au zoo,* and *Bonne nuit, ne mourez jamais*. She has performed in plays directed by Bruno Bayen, Gildas Bourdet, Eric Vigner, Mathhias Langhoff, Peter Sellars, and Joel Jouanneau. Her films and television credits include films directed by Philippe Le Guay, Philippe Monnier, Gérard Marx, Marcel Bluwal, and Pierre Boutron. Several of her radio plays were commissioned by France Culture: *Cartolandia, le déluge, Chupacabra Monceau, Petits précis d'instants péris*, winner of the Short Play Prize at the Radiophonies Festival, and *Radio Citrouille*, awarded the SACD Best Radio Talent Prize in 2006. Sigal was awarded a "Villa Medicis Hors les murs" grant in 1997, which allowed her to spend eight months in the United States, and a Mission Stendhal Fellowship in 2006, which she used to pursue her research and writing there.

Cole Swenson (translator, *A. W.O.L.*) is a noted poet and translator. She won the PEN American Award for her translation of *Island of the Dead* by Jean Fremon. A Guggenheim Fellow, she is also a member of the Academy of American Poets and teaches at the University of Iowa.

Michael Taormina (translator, *Cut*) is a scholar, translator, and poet. Most recently, he co-translated the second posthumous collection of interviews and essays by Gilles Deleuze, *Two Regimes of Madness* (Semiotexte). This follows on the heels of the first collection, *Desert Islands and Other Texts.* His world premiere translation of Ionesco's last play, *Journeys among the Dead*, was commissioned and performed by Division 13 Productions in 2003. He is currently an Assistant Professor of French at Hunter College, CUNY.

Michel Vinaver (playwright, *11 September 2001*) was born in Paris in 1927 and educated in France and the United States. Beginning in 1953, having already published two novels with Gallimard under the auspices of Albert Camus, he was hired by a multinational manufacturing corporation, Gillette. He wrote his first play, *Les Coréens*, in 1955, and thus began his journey as a writer and translator of theatre, which he pursued in tandem with his career in industry. From 1982 to 1991, he was also a teacher of theatrical studies at the University of Paris. His plays *Les Coréens, Les Huissiers, Iphigénie Hotel, Par-dessus Bord, La Demande d'emploi, A la renverse, L'Ordinaire*, and others have been translated and performed throughout the world and have been published in eight volumes under the title *Théâtre complet* (2002–2005) by Actes Sud and L'Arche Editeur in 2002 and 2003. In 2005, he agreed for the first time to direct one of his plays, *A la renverse*. His production ran for two months at the Théâtre des Athévains (Paris) in April-May 2006.

Philippa Wehle (editor; translator, *Inventories, Pumpkin on the Air, We Were Sitting on the Shores of the World . . .*) is Professor Emeritus of French Language and Culture and Drama Studies at Purchase College, State University of New York. She writes widely on contemporary theatre and performance and is the author of *Le Théâtre populaire selon Jean Vilar* (Actes Sud) and the editor of *DramaContemporary: France* (PAJ Publications). She has translated numerous contemporary French plays and is a Chevalier of the Order of Arts and Letters.